MARTHA
AND THE
DOCTOR

James W. Gally and his wife Martha in 1863, with their children
Matty and James (courtesy of B. Lewis).

MARTHA
AND THE
DOCTOR

A Frontier Family in Central Nevada

By
MARVIN LEWIS

Edited by B. Betty Lewis

A BRISTLECONE PAPERBACK
UNIVERSITY OF NEVADA PRESS
RENO, NEVADA 1977

Library of Congress Cataloging in Publication Data

Lewis, Marvin, 1923-1971.
    Martha and the Doctor.

    (A Bristlecone paperback)
    1. Gally, Martha. 2. Gally, James W.
3. Pioneers—Nevada—Biography. 4. Nevada—Frontier
and pioneer life. I. Title.
F841.L47   979.3'02'0924   [B]   77-24964
ISBN 0-87417-049-4

Grateful Acknowledgment is hereby made
to the Nevada American Revolution Bicentennial Commission
for their generous support of this book.

University of Nevada Press, Reno, Nevada 89557
© B. Betty Lewis 1977. All rights reserved
Book design by William H. Snyder
Cover design by John E. Sullivan
Printed in the United States of America

Contents

Preface

The frontier family occupies an obscure place in the history of westward expansion. Much has been recorded about the movement of people and the development of regions, but the integral social unit—the family—remains historically elusive. Of the hundreds of accounts pertaining to the gold and silver rushes, not many give an accurate portrayal of family life. The papers of the Gally family, which report on ten years of frontiering, stand as a major exception and open to view the way of life of an early family in the mining regions of central Nevada.

Much of the record of the Gally family is preserved in Martha Gally's diary, a frank and truthful account of her life. While this diary reveals the inner life of a frontier family, Dr. James W. Gally's surprisingly voluminous writings—stories, sketches, and letters—bring to life the everyday details of the small mining camps. Contained in the writings of both Dr. Gally and his wife, then, is not only their personal story of trials and tribulations, successes and defeats, adventuring and freedom, but also the story of frontier communities and the people who made them.

The Gallys were middle-class Americans from Zanesville, Ohio, where Dr. Gally had practiced dentistry for a number of years. Bitter political factionalism in Ohio (a result of the Civil War) led Dr. Gally to seek a new start in Iowa outside of Iowa City. He spent a year

farming a homestead there before he joined the ranks of
the California-bound emigrants.

The Gallys, en route to California from Iowa,
reached Austin, Nevada, an Overland Stage mining
settlement, on October 2, 1864, just a month before
Lincoln proclaimed Nevada a state. The Comstock Lode,
located in an eastern spur of the Sierra Nevada, was
nearing the end of its first five years of mining activity.
The intrepid prospectors had fanned out over the state,
and their reports of riches created excitement throughout
Nevada. The feverish expectations inspired the Gallys,
and they remained in Austin to participate in the mining
rushes that swept the eastern ranges of the state.

For ten years, the Gallys traveled the roads of central
and southeastern Nevada, restlessly searching for a stake
in the country. Living in isolated outposts, often far
removed from any kind of settlement, they experienced
loneliness, fear, misery, uncertainty, and poverty. Out of
these feelings, however, came communion with the land.
Dr. Gally was more exuberant than his wife about
Nevada, and he viewed his life in the state as his great
adventure.

Dr. Gally was a rough, uncut stone compared to
Martha's brother, George James, a successful lawyer and
man of affairs in Boston and the husband of Lilla Cabot
Lodge, the sister of Henry Cabot Lodge. Dr. Gally was,
however, an individualist and an intellectual in his own
right. Although he had been trained as a dentist, he gave
up his profession in Nevada and except for emergency
work had no regular practice. The restraints imposed by
society did not appeal to Dr. Gally, and he possessed the
courage to live his own life and to follow his ambitions
down many roads. He tried his hand at almost
everything—farming, prospecting, hauling, brickmaking,

mining—but he loved best politicking and writing.

He had the gifts to make a name for himself in writing, but he scattered his energies in many other directions. The amount of unpaid work he did for newspapers and periodicals was considerable. Newspapers in Nevada published over the years his poems, stories, essays, and letters under the pseudonym of "Singleline." The idea for the pen name came from the practice of driving long teams of mules or horses with a single line, an act which served as a symbol of skill for him as he drove his pen across the page. He was much more widely known as an author under his pseudonym than under his real name.

As a perceptive, intelligent man, Dr. Gally wrote about frontier people and the mining communities of Nevada in an original manner. Dr. Gally captured in his sketches the essence of the daily lives of prospectors, miners, and teamsters. He was intrigued not so much by the wildness of a booming camp and the lurid exploits that were usually reported in the newspapers, but rather by the unique consciousness of the Nevada silver boom era.

Singleline's pen portraits of Nevada and its odd frontier characters reflect his awareness of this consciousness. He knew the prospectors and the teamsters because he had been one of them. He had tramped over much of southeastern Nevada observing carefully its terrain and resources. He had talked Nevada politics, had run for public office, and had been a justice of the peace. He knew the Nevada barroom, which offered newspapers and periodicals on the tables, good talk on every subject, and a warm place to stop for brandy on a cold day. He had a romantic attachment to the sagebrush country and its people. The defeats and the disappointments did not crush him, for there seemed to be so much reason for hope.

Partly by accident and partly by intent, the Gallys had been swept into a movement that belonged to the great tide of continental migration. They were uniquely prepared to preserve a segment of that story. The migrant folk whom they represented—acquisitive, long-suffering, and enduring—have traveled for decades the great highway of American history.

Acknowledgments

I was first introduced to James W. Gally through Duncan Emrich's collection of pieces by Nevada writers, a work entitled *Comstock Bonanza*. Emrich's enthusiasm for Dr. Gally's writings was contagious, and he encouraged me to research the man and his work.

The search for materials and information about the Gally family has been aided by many individuals and institutions. I am grateful to Dr. John B. Bisbee, the grandson of Martha and James W. Gally, who gave me background information about the Gally family and who was helpful in every step of preparing the manuscript. Dr. Bisbee and his cousins, Mrs. Robert Daniel Thompson and Mrs. Elmer Eaton Jordan of San Francisco, generously gave the Gally Family Papers to the Bancroft Library, making them accessible to the public.

Several individuals offered me special assistance in my research. My appreciation is extended to Allan R. Ottley of the California State Library; David F. Myrick of San Francisco; and particularly Dr. John B. Tompkins, Helen Bretnor, and the staff of the Bancroft Library. Robert H. Becker, assistant director of the Bancroft Library, saw the value of the Gally Family Papers and his interest made possible the preservation of a family's view of frontier life in Nevada.

In collecting data about the Gallys, I have benefited from Norris F. Schneider's fund of knowledge about

Zanesville, Ohio. Mr. Everett Greer of Zanesville also was able to supply some interesting information about James W. Gally's older brother, Thomas. This information led me to surviving members of James Gally's wife's family, the James family.

I thank the editors of *Western Humanities Review* and *Nevada Historical Society Quarterly* for permission to make extensive use of material from my articles in those journals ("James W. Gally and Frontier Culture: A Forgotten Representative," *Western Humanities Review*, X [Spring 1956] and "Hot Creek and the Wide Gray Valley," *Nevada Historical Society Quarterly*, XIII [Summer 1970]).

* * *

My brother died before the final revision of the manuscript could be completed. His work consequently required editorial assistance from various sources. I wish to express my gratitude to Robert Laxalt, director of the University of Nevada Press, for his generous encouragement and invaluable assistance. His helpful criticism enabled me to utilize more fully Martha Gally's diary entries and Dr. Gally's letters and newspaper articles, all of which reflect a relatively unknown side of Nevada's frontier era. Mr. Laxalt edited Chapter 14 and skillfully deleted those sections that were not pertinent to mining camp life. I appreciate Dr. William Hanchett's kindness in offering helpful suggestions and authenticating the information on the Fourteenth Amendment in Chapter 5. My thanks also to Dean Charles Breese, editorial board member, who read and commented on the manuscript.

San Diego   B. LEWIS
January 1977

1

cA Backward Glance

WITH THE early spring of 1864, as the ground thawed and the sun warmed the earth, the Gally family prepared to leave Iowa for the long journey to California. The year before, they had come from Ohio with high hopes of developing a homestead on the outskirts of Iowa City. A premature frost and cold weather in early September, however, had ruined the crops they had planted in the spring.

Before coming to Iowa City, the Gallys had lived in Zanesville, Ohio. During eight years of married life there, they had known considerable security and happiness. They could look with pride and satisfaction on their children: James, born in 1856, and Matty, born in 1858. Dr. Gally had built up a good dental practice in the town. Professionally established, he had bought into the Zanesville *Aurora* in 1856, and the following year became its sole publisher and editor.

For the eighth son of immigrant Irish parents, James W. Gally had done exceedingly well. His parents, John Gally and Jane Mulligan, had come to America in 1812 from County Cavan in northern Ireland. After a number of moves, they followed the tide of immigration down the Ohio River to Wheeling, West Virginia. When they arrived in Wheeling in 1817, fewer than fifteen hundred people lived there. By the time James was twenty-four, it was a bustling town of more than thirteen thousand people and had the distinction of being an active industrial center that produced a variety of articles: nails, cabinet-ware, copper, tin, sheet iron, carriages and wagons, glass, iron castings, plows, and bricks.[1]

John Gally worked hard to establish himself in America and eventually owned a brickmaking business which prospered. Life in America evoked two responses in the Gallys: a patient struggle with circumstances and a quest for self-improvement. Although John Gally had seen the typical dream of immigrant success come true, he wanted more for his children than he had achieved for himself. His two youngest sons, Thomas and James, were gifted intellectually, and Thomas, in particular, was the pride of his family. James wrote of him: "An impulsive generous heart and brilliant intellect gave him a high place among honorable men—he sought for a higher place but met in death the solemn truth: 'There is nothing great but God.'"[2] The same high aspiration motivated James.

As a practical matter, the task of earning a living was solved when James chose a career in dentistry. His apprenticeship was served under Dr. S. P. Hullihen, a well-known Wheeling dentist. At the end of three years of study, he decided to set up a practice elsewhere. The son of a man who had converted from Catholicism to Methodism, he believed fervently in opportunity, progress, and freedom. Hidden away in his own consciousness, and muted for a short time, were the powerful impulses that impelled him to turn his back on conventional respectability and success. But first, he chose the road to Zanesville.

The doctor arrived in Zanesville in 1852 at the age of twenty-five. About seventy-five miles from Wheeling, Zanesville was a thriving manufacturing city in which rail lines from central Ohio and Cleveland intersected. Its population at the close of the 1850s was thirteen thousand. For a young man who needed a start, Zanesville was a promising place that was not too far from home. The young doctor set up his office on Main Street opposite the city hall, and advertised his skill as a dentist, backed up by a recommendation from Dr. Hullihen. In a few years, he was established and practicing with a partner, George Crawford. [3]

James Gally's professional position in Zanesville gave him carte blanche into the social life of the town. One of its leading families was that of George James, who was a successful lawyer and who played a leading role in civic affairs. [4] He had built a fine brick residence in which he and his wife and their several children lived in middle-class comfort. George James was especially proud of his oldest daughter, Martha (Mat), who was one of the most attractive belles in Zanesville.

Mat James grew up in a happy home, one that she recalled fondly and warmly. During the hard years of pioneering, the memory of this home would make her ache with a sense of loss. George James was well-to-do, having built up investments in real estate, bonds, mortgages, and other property. Thus, Mat was brought up in the midst of material plenty and warm affection. Though some people in Zanesville felt that George James had a "hasty and virulent temper," [5] the doors of his house were always open, and "cordial, abundant hospitality" was proffered.

The sitting room was the contentment of Mat James's childhood, and she always remembered the comfort of the rocking chair and lounge and the attraction of the many books shelved in "their incongruous cases." The walls were lined with maps and pictures, including one of Uncle Broaddus who was "monarch of the mantle wall" and one of Uncle John, who seemed "a wonder of beauty" with his happy, eminent face. A large round table was covered with many objects, and between the windows, a stand—which the children called a "pedestal"—was laden at all times with apples. The only discordant element consisted of "those ugly rattling slats of blinds." To complete this island of happiness was Mat's mother, who seemed "so loving, serene & sufficient, so tender for husband and child."[6]

The death of Martha Abbott James left a vacuum in the lives of her children. Mat gave some idea of the depth of her own feelings at her mother's death in a letter written in later years to her brother George:

> Oh George we had a happy home! & such a mother—we shall never look upon her like again. Today, by the merest accident I took up a garment that I knew she had darned & my eyes blinded & my heart choked when I thought of her dear fingers & all her watchful care & patient kindness to us children. If she only might come back again I would be a better child to her. I love her truer & deeper every year & the meaning of her precepts & examples checks many a hasty word & uncharitable thought.[7]

James Gally had married Martha James three years before her mother's death. Evenly matched in interests and cultivation, they had a romantic love affair. Mat had a cultivated mind that enjoyed the play of ideas and the refinements of civilized society. Her love of books, plays, and family life, coupled with a sprightly imagination, permitted her to select and retain those ideas that could be embodied in a conversation or letter. The more subtle differences in the couple's backgrounds did not emerge until after marriage.

For several years, life passed for James and Mat with the usual successes, trials, and tribulations. A major, sombre event, however, marked the early years of marriage. In 1860, the third child born to them died in his second month of life, from whooping cough. Each year Mat recalled in her diary the baby's passing, and shortly after his son's death, Dr. Gally expressed his feelings in a poem entitled, "My Little Boy is Dead." One verse reads:

> Yet I would not feel again,—
> Though I sorrow through the pain
> Which is swirling in my brain
> Nearly wild—
> No! I would not feel anew
> Like to those who never knew
> Their own child.[8]

With the finality of the loss fixed in his mind, he showed insight into man's subconscious thought in a four-line inscription to "little King":

> What we know we comprehend
> What we do not know we imagine
> The image in the brain is no
> less an idol than the sculptured stone.[9]

The sense of personal tragedy for the Gallys was muted by the events leading up to the Civil War. As editor and publisher of the *Aurora*, Dr. Gally's editorial opinions plunged him into the acrimonious politics that marked the end of the decade. He was not a pro-slavery fire-eater, but a moderate who had shifted his allegiance from the Whig party of Henry Clay to the Democratic party.[10]

People in Ohio on the eve of the Civil War were split in their loyalties between the Douglass and Breckinridge wings of the Democratic party. There was strong feeling that constitutional rights gave legality to slavery in the South, and this clamor over constitutional rights imparted to the pro-slavery cause a moral fervor that otherwise would have been lacking. Dr. Gally exemplified the view that legality gave to slavery a dimension of righteousness. In 1859, for example, he editorialized against the Market Street Baptist Church for its part in denouncing unrighteous laws; he did not want to see "the cross of Christ throw odium upon our laws."[11] "We held the constitution," wrote Gally in 1871, "to be paramount, and we were convinced, from the first, that the Republicans meant emancipation, and we knew that Congressional-Executive emancipation was not constitutional."[12]

The argument over constitutional rights obscured the basic motives for pro-slavery advocacy. After the Civil War, when Dr. Gally had time to think dispassionately about the politics of the war years, he admitted candidly that he had held pro-slavery views, "not for the love or profit of slavery to me or mine, but because I thought the system of slavery was the strongest legal social barrier between the poorest white and the richest black."[13] Gally, like many other men on the opposite side of the fence, feared the Negro. Free-Soilers and northern Democrats alike did not want the Negro competing in an environment that already was rife with individual competitive pressures. Actually, Dr. Gally's strong attachment to the cause of the free white man should have made him a Free-Soiler, but family ties in his native state of Virginia and marriage into a family with strong southern sympathies were decisive factors in molding his viewpoint.

Four months after Gally sold the *Aurora* on April 13, 1863, a pro-Breckinridge sheet, the *Citizen's Press*, commenced publication in its place. A mob of indignant Zanesville citizens who protested its pro-slavery, pro-South politics attacked the building where it was published.[14] Although political animosities were exploding around him, the meaning of civil conflict was not brought home to Dr. Gally until November 1861 when Mat's cousin, Butler Abbott, was killed. Christmas 1861 was abounding in new tribulations and more were to come.

Dr. Gally was an avowed follower of Clement Vallandigham, an Ohio Democrat who was seeking a negotiated peace. He felt that the war was strangling civil liberties and his campaign was designed to disrupt recruiting. General Burnside, who had been given command of the Department of Ohio, reasoned that Vallandigham was a traitor and ordered him arrested and imprisoned. On April 13, 1863, Burnside issued as a war measure "General Order Number 38," which suspended the First Amendment to the Constitution. Even a declaration of sympathy for the rebels was not to be countenanced, and death was to be the punishment for a person convicted of treason.

Before the release of this official order, dissenters were punished by individual and mob action. As examples of this, the editor of the Dayton *Empire*, J. F. Bollmeyer, a "Peace Democrat," was murdered by a pro-Unionist man in 1862. And members of the James family, who were secessionist in their sympathies, were called names in the street, and at the door of their house they were denounced as "Copperheads." With official repression, however, the dissenters were more effectively muzzled and were forced to run for cover.

Shortly after arriving in Nevada, in a letter to his father-in-law, Gally alluded to politics and described himself as a "wandering citizen," an unenviable state of being into which he had been forced by the suspension of constitutional rights.[15] Gally had probably objected, with the other Copperheads, to the curtailment of the writ of habeas corpus in Ohio and the opportunity it gave for the "political, unclean birds" to twist words. In Gally's opinion, there were several of these individuals in Zanesville. To his father-in-law he poured out his bitterness:

> When you write again please, if not too much trouble,
> tell me if that old arch hypocrite Deputy Treasurer John
> Dillon has gone to Hell yet or "shuffled off his mortal
> coil" preliminary thereto. How is the hopeful Applegate
> family—has its general rotteness not yet culminated. How
> is the saintly Daniel Brush who murdered Billy Lynn by
> the slow tortures of financial lying. Oh! the Cat with his
> soft-paws and his balmy love for the Lord Jesus—if he or
> I do not live forever and there is a final judgment, you
> will be there and Billy Lynn will be there, and I will be
> called up from the court below to testify in the case of
> Kingdom of Heaven vs D. Brush et al—a case wherein
> the Defendants claim to be heirs of Jesus Christ—you
> will see then by what the attorney for the Plf draws out
> of Mr. Lynn that old Daniel Brush is a d----d old
> scoundrel and old John Dillon is his Judas Iscariot.
> Excuse my profanity, but if it had not been for this war I
> should have devoted 5 years of my life to a prosecution
> of that nest of treasury thieves. How is Bob Crow? Bill
> Mason? Marsh? Marsh is not a rascal—only a beast. How
> is Haines? Haines is a fool who never forgave me for
> showing up at Adamsville. I do not hate Marsh or
> Haines—tools are to be pitied, not hated. How is
> Potwire? I see, by papers, that Muse flourishes like a

blue bottle-fly at a butcher stall—actively stealing and blowing. How is Charley Russell my regards to him he was to me ever a gentleman.[16]

The doctor might have endured the bitter hatreds of the war years as others did, but the tug of a new start was too powerful to resist. The opportunity to leave Zanesville came when George James deeded to Mat Gally and her brother, Richard Fuller James, joint ownership of some undivided farm property in Iowa. This fateful offer changed the course of the family's life.

2

The Emigrant Road

For the Gallys, homesteading in Iowa was a transitional step in their westward journey. Their future hopes and plans had depended on a successful harvest, but prairie farming offered only heartbreak and disappointment. There would have been five or six hundred bushels of potatoes had not the frost frozen the vines black. After struggling through the winter in Iowa, the Gallys became intrigued by the widespread talk about emigrating to California.

Mat wheedled her father and wrung from him permission to sell the land he had deeded to them and to Fuller, Mat's brother. They sold the property for $1,820, with $1,220 down and the balance in notes paid a few days before their departure for California. The Gallys held Fuller's share of the money from the sale of the land, and they agreed reluctantly to include him in their emigrant party. With nothing now to hold them, they joined the emigrant wagons moving West.

The Gallys left Iowa in April of 1864 with fifteen horses, three wagons, and two cows. Dr. Gally was the captain of a small party consisting of eight men and five wagons.[1] This small company merged with a hundred thousand other emigrants, many of them—like the Gallys—pro-Southern in their sympathies.

After crossing the Missouri River, the company began the long haul along the Platte River in Nebraska. In the Platte Valley, the emigrants complained often of the scarcity of fuel, and they sometimes had to burn weeds and buffalo chips. In addition, the dry winds and heat made each day's journey miserable. Dr. Gally remembered 1864 as the year of the drouth,[2] and a frontier army officer said the wind in the middle of July "came over the baked plains dry and lifeless."[3] Eyes smarted from the sand and alkali. The ever-present mosquitoes and buffalo gnats added to the discomfort. Martha despaired at the many mounds of earth marking the remains of the children who had died on the march, and the sight of the "little graves" made her think of the mound at home. "I thanked God," she wrote later to her father, "if my little mound was alone it was at home among you all."[4] Fortunately, the Gallys were in good physical health as they threaded their way over the plains.

By 1864, emigrant travel had attained a certain level of perfection. Replacement parts were carried along for the wagons, as well as all kinds of equipment and tools including axes, hatchets, spades, sewing articles, matches, and a medicine chest. Bacon, preserved in hundred-pound sacks and insulated with bran in boxes, served as the staple item of food. Stations and ranches, purveying supplies and services, were located at intervals of from one to fifteen miles all the way up the Platte Valley to the

Rocky Mountains. Overloading wagons was not necessary when groceries, grain, and hardware could be bought on the trail.[5]

Travel along the Platte River was heavy. Long trains, comprised of as many as eight hundred ox teams, were counted passing one ranch in a single day. These trains were made up of many separate outfits and sometimes were strung out from ten to fifteen miles. Heavily laden Mormon trains, with many foreign immigrants attached to them, also moved along the trail.

The 1864 plains emigration was hotly contested by the Indians. During the spring, General Mitchell had come to Fort Cottonwood to convince the Sioux to keep away from the Platte Valley. Nothing much came of this request, and in subsequent meetings the Indians refused to make a settlement. They opposed white encroachments into the country north of the Platte River while the Cheyenne and Arapahoe were increasingly protesting white incursions south of the Platte. The crisis abated somewhat when Spotted Tail moved his band into the Big Horn country. Trouble still came, however, from dissident young braves who organized hit-and-run war parties for the purpose of stealing the emigrants' stock and possessions. The Cheyenne and Arapahoe could no longer be restrained either, and as the summer lengthened, emigrants became aware of their presence along the Smoky Hill route between Kansas and Denver.

At the height of the season, the entire route of the Platte Valley came under increasingly heavier Indian incursions and depredations. Quite early in the summer, the hundred miles between Fort Kearney and Fort Cottonwood offered considerable danger. On the bluffs overlooking the ranches, small bands of Cheyennes were sighted. Reports from north of the river told of Brulé Sioux war dances. One dramatic incident involving the Indians occurred in May. Soldiers stationed at Fort Cottonwood, not far from where the town of North Platte is located today, were looking toward the north bank of the river, when they saw a whiff of smoke, a burning wagon, and stampeding horses. The Indians attacked suddenly within view of the post in broad daylight, killed two men, and escaped with their booty.[6] In July, the sight of burned-out wagons west of Julesburg did not come as a shock. Ranchers abandoned their land over the 250 miles between the forks of the Platte River and Fort Laramie, as the Indians waited for opportunities to fall on the emigrants throughout the territory.

It took all of Dr. Gally's presence of mind to keep his party from falling prey to a surprise attack. As they moved along the Platte River, they saw constant reminders of Indian depredations: people killed and wagons burned. As the Gally party made its way, traveling perhaps ten to twenty miles per day, all eyes were constantly alert for prowling bands of Sioux and Cheyenne. The horses could not be rested for any length of time because of fear of an attack. Not much grass was available on the plains, but the little that was available had to be passed up because of the hazards. The expense of buying feed along the way drained Dr. Gally's purse, but worse yet was the poor condition of the horses fagged out by the relentless drive. Five of his horses were so run-down that he would eventually lose them in Nevada.

Something of the confusion and uncertainty of travel evoked by Indian war parties was evident by midsummer at Julesburg. At this town, the road to Denver branched off to the south, while the main Salt Lake trail bore to the north and west. By July 22, there were three miles of wagon trains awaiting the arrival of troops before crossing the South Platte River to proceed along the Salt Lake trail. The ''pilgrims'' were having a hard time of it, trying to find grass for their stock and arguing with one another during the delay. At last, the military gave the order for the trains to move and actively supervised the river crossing. Quicksand made the exercise extremely hazardous, and a firm route across the river was essential. To move wagons ahead with all possible speed, the mules were urged forward by shouts and oaths. Late into the night the wagons crossed the river, while men with lanterns illuminated the water on both sides of the moving wagons.[7]

The road now headed to Fort Laramie through country that was ''absolutely wild.'' Near Chimney Rock (a formation rising three hundred feet above the valley floor) the brilliant transparency of the atmosphere and the purity of the air were exhilarating. Not even the presence of several burned wagons on the ridges detracted from the ebullient feeling of health and well-being of the emigrants. Farther on, wild sheep were seen in the vicinity of Scott's Bluff. The final stretch of the journey to Fort Laramie was over sandhills and through deep dust.

Shortly past Fort Laramie, the emigrant trains wended through the foothill country of the Laramie Mountains. The steep hills, strewn with rocks and boulders, created difficult terrain, and the alkali water did not agree with the cattle.[8] Somewhere in the foothill country, the Gallys had their most disastrous encounter with Indians. Three men in their party, the owners of a four-mule team, had fallen behind the main party at the beginning of the day's trek. Before ten o'clock, the

Indians had pounced on them. Carelessness cost these men their team, but as Dr. Gally wrote in a letter to his father-in-law, it was difficult to enforce strict rules of march:

> The great trouble I had was to get people who never had been attacked by Indians to realize the situation because you do not see the Indian at all when he is bent on hostilities until he is upon you with a whoop, a flight of arrows, and balls; then if you take flight he takes what he wants and leaves you with your foot in your hand a long way from hope or assistance: if you resist he overpowers you if he can, but if he cannot he keeps upon your track to be revenged for his people whom you may have maimed or killed.[9]

Along the trail, news of mishap and misfortune traveled fast. Several days after the long line of wagons had crossed the North Platte River near Julesburg, an emigrant family of seven ran into trouble in the vicinity of Deer Creek, west of Fort Laramie. The father of the family was carelessly handling a firearm and killed himself with an accidental discharge of the weapon. His wife, Mrs. Ringo, brought her five children, two wagons, oxen, and mules without mishap to Austin, where they arrived four days after the Gallys.[10] The possibility of a tragedy of this kind weighed heavily on all emigrant families.

Once over the South Pass, there was no longer any danger of Indian raids. The wagon trains headed for Fort Bridger through the Bitter Creek country, a land of little water and poor feed. At the fort, the emigrants rested their stock and bought needed supplies at the sutler's store.

The remaining miles to Salt Lake City traversed a jumbled mass of mountain ranges,[11] but as the wagons crawled out of Parley's Canyon, ''through an opening, almost like an immense doorway, unarched at the top,"[12] a pleasing sight greeted the emigrants. The Mormons had irrigated the canyons, and the emerald hue of growing things contrasted with the monotony of the desert. Grain fields, herds of cattle, laden barns, and humming windmills were evidences of prosperity and civilization. Although the farms looked rich and carefully tended, the private houses were unpretentious and common-looking. Most were made of wood or slab; the better ones resembled bungalows and the poorer ones were not much more than huts. In the center of the town, the Mormon leaders had their houses, the most ostentatious being Governor Young's house. The Salt Lake House, the leading hotel, rented rooms at reasonable prices, and the largest Gentile (non-Mormon) business establishments were located on Main Street. The Mormons had planted trees along parallel, laid-out streets carrying running water in ditches, but they had not bothered to build sidewalks.

Salt Lake City had about fourteen thousand inhabitants in 1860. Pauperism hardly existed in Utah, with real wealth concentrated in land, livestock, and farming implements. In addition, more than a million dollars was invested in manufacturing. The emigrant discovered quickly that there was an abundance of goods for sale at moderate prices, and the shops on Main Street carried fineries of every description. The high freight rates forced up prices on imported goods, but the staple items could be bought reasonably.[13]

To the emigrant, who had still to travel over the desert, Salt Lake City was an oasis in the long trek. The worst drawback for the frontier American was the absence of public saloons, but liquor could be bought at a city-operated store. The notion of polygamy was also a problem for many Americans. One intelligent traveler expressed what was a common attitude of those days: "But here are hundreds and thousands of women deceived into an infamous captivity, held as slaves by the most fanatical prejudices, and nothing is done to alleviate their sufferings or to rescue them from an earthly death."[14]

After stopping in Salt Lake City, the Gallys entered Nevada at the end of August. The pervasive silence of the land impressed Dr. Gally as his eye followed the receding line of the wagon road to the far horizon. He recorded his impressions of the weird wildness of the land in a description entitled "Out in the Night":

> In October; in Nevada; the clear, steely, cold, Autumnal sky; the dry, rolling, valley-undulations of gravel and sand; the far-off hills of gray, the farther hills of black, the farthest peaks of snow-white altitudes fencing in the dull yellowish sombre scenery; all silent save where the raven, with the regular swith-swith, swith-swith, of his coal-black wing, veers his bee-line flight among the red-tipped arrows of the setting sun; nothing to remind a civilized man of any of his antecedents, unless the long wavering line of ribbon-like wagon road, with its wheel tracks of last week, leading from the wainwright dustily onward to the limbs of lost vehicles may be a faint suggestion that man is orderly and mechanical in other lands beyond the hills—in countries where no whirling spiral of electric atoms play along the highway, an illusive mimicry of the "pillar of cloud by day."[15]

The doctor's family was familiar with the life, change, motion, and color of the Mississippi Valley; the sagebrush land was a far departure from the sap and verdure of their old home. All was strangely quiet in the valleys, save for the occasional sound of a hare, a bluejay, or a raven; and after the sunlit hours, the sombre shadows lengthened into forlorn darkness reinforced by the "shivering howl" of a coyote. To Dr. Gally, it seemed like a ghostly world, a haunted domain. As they made their evening camp on the floor of a sagebrush valley, they had reason to contemplate the "dead silence." "Back home (as we fondly call the old States)," Dr. Gally wrote in 1870, "there is snow or there is not snow; but here, one stands at night on the dry sand in the valley, or lies on his blankets among the dusky gray of the bushes, while a little way from him, on either hand, the snowy peaks, white as the ghostly warders in a fairy tale, keep stern and shrouded guard upon the scene."[16]

The Gallys had to cross mountain ranges that ran short distances in broken but nearly parallel formations on their way to Austin. The ranges enclosed valley floors and abounded in sinks, marshes, alkali flats, and passes, many of the passes leaving delightful impressions on the travelers.[17] About fifty miles from the Utah border was Schellbourne Pass and the Schell Creek Station. This was a pleasant stopping place because it afforded cold spring water. Egan Canyon, the pass that connected Steptoe and Butte valleys, offered scenery "wildly grand and beautiful"; clumps of willow trees gave welcome shade in the summer months, and in season wild roses and gooseberries grew profusely and many doves made the canyon their nesting territory.

On the evening of September 2, the Gallys camped on the western slope of the Egan Range. The Butte Range, separating Butte and Long valleys, amazed the travelers with its wild beauty: the growth of mahogany trees and the abundant foliage generated comparison with Bierstadt's "Mount Hood," or Church's "Heart of the

Andes." Hastings' Pass, at 6,789 feet above sea level, now named Overland Pass, cut through the Ruby Mountains and was enjoyed for its beauty. On the other side of the range, the South Fork of the Humboldt River flowed northward to join the main river west of present-day Elko. From Jacob's Well at the headwaters of the South Fork to Austin was a hundred miles, with the Diamond, Sulphur Springs, Roberts Creek, and Toiyabe ranges yet to be crossed.

The Gally family enjoyed the newness of the sagebrush land. They traveled in a leisurely manner, taking a month to cover the 157 miles from Egan Canyon to Austin in central Nevada. Both men and animals benefited by the slower pace of the march. The Gallys felt invigorated by the dry, warm, autumn climate. This lap of the journey would have been entirely pleasant had not a disagreeable rift developed between Mat's brother, Fuller, and Dr. Gally.

The friction between the two, which had caused problems in Iowa, was intensified during the most difficult part of the journey up the Platte Valley. Fuller had panicked in Indian country, and was accused by Dr. Gally of being cowardly, lazy, and irresponsible. Another quarrel occurred when they reached Salt Lake. Mat reported to her father that the doctor wanted to part with Fuller at that place: "At Salt Lake the Dr. told F. 'I want you to come with me to the Express Office have me send your Greenbacks to your Father & you either go after them, stay here, or what you please. I have dragged you through the Indians at some expense of body, mind & pride & now I'm done.'"[18] The choices the doctor gave Fuller were hardly fair ones, but perhaps he wanted to frighten Fuller into a kind of rectitude. Without the money that belonged to him and without any other visible means of support, Fuller would be stranded. The prospect of returning alone across the plains in 1864 would not appeal to an experienced frontiersman, let alone a greenhorn such as Fuller. Fuller ran to his sister and implored her with "his usual tears" to make the doctor relent. She upbraided him for his lack of pride, but the upshot was that the Gallys took Fuller along with them.

Little changed in the relationship between the two men, however, and sixty miles from Austin the doctor lost all patience with Fuller and for some offense or other threw him to the ground. Fuller, who was physically much larger than the doctor, did not fight back, but he was humiliated sufficiently to ask for the loan of a pistol at a nearby cabin. His request was refused, and badly piqued, he started for Austin in the company of two Englishmen who had been borrowing food from the Gallys. The next they saw of Fuller was in Austin, where he appeared with a lawyer who claimed the Gallys' entire train. The doctor was furious and was nearly on the verge of assaulting Fuller a second time. Mat intervened, had the lawyer bring Fuller to her, and forced Fuller to acknowledge the untruth of his claim. At this point, "the lawyer told him he was a great liar & left. F. cried said he was awful hungry," and was taken into the tent and given a meal.[19] Dr. Gally gave him some money to buy blankets, and Fuller joined a wagon train bound for Sacramento. The bulk of the $900 belonging to Fuller from the sale of his share of the Iowa land remained in the doctor's hands.

The Gallys had come to the end of their emigrant road—the beginning of the second chapter of their pioneer adventure. For the doctor, this was a time of expectation.

His boundless energy would expend itself in many pursuits. The children would become seasoned in the ways of a new life, but for their mother, there existed mixed emotions. Her nervous energy, drained by the plains crossing; a sense of guilt about her brother Fuller; and doubts and fears about their future overwhelmed her. The days and years to come were to bear out some of her darkest premonitions. They had escaped the arrows of the Indians to discover the wilderness of Nevada.

The strange remoteness of the sagebrush country, the vast expanse, the mirages, and the rugged cliffs and mountains made the doctor feel that Nevada was the "Hagar of Nature, the Desert's child." Skillfully, he captured the essence of frontier Nevada in his poem, "Nevada," published in 1869 about four years after he had arrived in Austin. It caught the appeal of the sagebrush state to a generation of frontiersmen and expressed the vision that led them on the long, hard adventure: The song of their quest is central to Dr. Gally's life in Nevada.

> The air is dry
> And the day is new,
> With not a drop of the sparkling dew
> To rust the dawning arrows that fall
> Over the mountain's western wall:
> For this is Nevada,
> The weird and wild;
> The Hagar of Nature,
> The Desert's child;
> Ragged and dusty,
> Tawny and torn,
> Waiting for warmth
> At the gates of morn.

Ismael comes of her,
Striding his steed;
Out of the homes of her,
Taking no heed;
Wild as the Aloween,
Seeking for pelf,
Caring for nought, I ween,
Not for himself.
Like the wild coyote
That howls o'er the plain,
Here he is, there he is, once and again—
What he gets heeds he not,
Never keeps what is got;
Ease is unknown to him,
Life is alone, to him,
   Rustle and go.

Houses he has, and had;
Cabins, both good and bad,
Friends at the East and a hope at "the Bay";
But he must wander here,
Bustle and squander here,
Mountain-wild Arab, he can't stay away;
Wealth ever haunts him
And poverty taunts him;
His mule and his saddle and spurs are at hand;
Where there's a show for it
There he must "go for it,"
Thus he rides recklessly over the land.[20]

cA New Country

O<small>N OCTOBER</small> 2, 1864, the Gallys camped on the summit of the Toiyabe Range of mountains, with the town of Austin in the canyon to the west of them. Many emigrant parties rested their stock here, for feed and water cost nothing. The days were warm, the sky was cloudless and sparkling blue, but the nights were cool—characteristics of autumn in Nevada.

The Gallys had to decide what to do next: recruit their stock and proceed on to California, or remain in Austin for the winter as some emigrants were doing. Mat was exhausted from the trip, the stock was run-down, and the cost of buying feed along the way was reported to be high. Emotionally drained by the trip and the quarrels with Fuller, the Gallys decided to remain in Austin through the winter.

Austin, the principal town of the Reese River Mining District and the county seat of Lander County, occupies the upper reaches of a canyon on the western slope of the

Toiyabe Range. At the entrance to the precipitous canyon, a settlement known as Clifton sprang up before Austin came into existence. The people who came in 1862 and 1863 stripped the hillsides of their growth and hurriedly erected cabins of nut pine and granite. The slopes, disfigured by the stumps of the scrubby pine, were then worked over by prospectors, who left hundreds of pockmarked excavation mounds. The setting had a sagebrush picturesqueness: the nearly barren hills framed by the long empty line of the Reese River Valley in the distance.

Austin was a bustling place when the Gallys arrived. A steady flow of traffic from California and Salt Lake made its way through the town, for it was not only a major mining settlement in Nevada, but it was also situated on the transcontinental road. The emigrant trains, the overland stage lines, and the express outfits had layovers there; and the telegraph line linked Austin with both coasts. A main street, intersected by cross streets climbing over the hills, was jammed with traffic during the peak daylight hours. Frame buildings, for the most part carefully constructed, lined both sides of Main Street. Most of the residential houses were built of adobe, but wood, burnt brick, sagebrush, and canvas were used as well.[1]

Although Austin had all the rudimentary signs of civilization when the Gallys arrived, two years before there had been nothing but a stone cabin in the canyon. The winter of 1862-63 saw parties camping in tents on snow-blanketed ground. Supplies and provisions came in during the spring and summer months; the canyon was graded, making it passable to wagons; a hotel was opened, and a newspaper was founded. The money for these projects came from the owners of town lots and other interested enterprisers who had pooled their resources in a town company. At the cost of several thousand dollars, the town company had shifted the center of trade from Clifton on the flat at the mouth of the canyon to Austin on the slopes of the Toiyabe. After the grade was completed, the Clifton settlement became the center of milling operations.[2]

The hypnotic power of a mining boom was reflected in the number of claims, the speculative fever, and the fantastic dreams of wealth.[3] The speculative craze discouraged outside investment during the later months of 1863. It was not until the spring of 1864, with the extraction of rich-paying ore from the Oregon ledges and the introduction of a roasting process for refractory ores in the Vanderbosch Mill, that capital began to arrive from San Francisco.

What justified confidence in Nevada mining was the richness of the silver-bearing ore veins, encased in the granite of the hills and running in asymmetrical formation. Although these veins were not particularly large (varying from three inches to three or four feet in width) they were rich in silver chemically bound to sulphurets, antimony, and arsenic.

The initial opening of mines was the work of poor men who, by their persistence, had proved the worth of the district's mineral deposits.[4] But advanced metallurgical processes were required to reduce this type of ore, and capital and mills were needed desperately. Even as late as the middle of 1865, there were not more than a half dozen mills reducing the ore extracted from fifty veins. Miners could send to these mills only the richest ores, as the price of mining and milling was $100 a ton. Many miners resorted to hand mortars and hand machinery to reduce small quantities of ore. By 1865, Eastern capital was attracted to Reese River, and mines were selling at prices ranging from $10,000 to $100,000.[5] Except for a major break during the winter of 1865, the Reese River mines were the most productive in eastern Nevada until challenged by those of White Pine in 1868.

Austin had benefited from the enthusiasm generated by a substantial number of community builders. In the summer of 1863, a courageous woman opened a school in a brush tent; by the beginning of 1864, Austinites had provided the money to establish a fire company; and in the months to come, civic-minded men eloquently discussed the needs of the community. Like other mining booms, however, the Reese River rush also had created social disorder. Drunkenness, disorderly conduct, and a homicide now and then ranked as the most common offenses. Several months before the Gallys arrived, a city government had come into existence; a mayor, clerk, recorder, marshal, assessor, and aldermen had been elected in mid-April. With the creation of a city government, hope ran high that the rough element in the town would be held in check.

The work of the Common Council even at best followed a haphazard course. The council received numerous requests to repair the streets, but action was slow in coming. The lack of sidewalks and gutters definitely was a problem, as Main Street was often muddy when water leaked into it from the reservoir. In the latter part of October, the Common Council voted $1,000 to make repairs; but they then discovered an inadequate treasury, traced to the nonpayment of taxes by eight hundred citizens against whom the city attorney had tardily commenced to move. Some people advised the city fathers to use the labor of these same delinquent taxpayers to improve the streets.[6]

The city fathers were besieged by other plaguing developments indicating private and public indifference. Abandoned wagons stood in "broken squads and solid ranks through our streets," and piles of manure and filth stood in the public thoroughfare. Stable owners were disposing of manure by hauling it to the upper grade and dumping it there, to the extreme annoyance of everyone's nostrils. Meanwhile, the town's marshal avoided the unpleasant subject and the wrongdoers. Furthermore, the blacksmiths—by fueling large fires which threw off cinders and ash outside their shops—created a fire hazard endangering nearby dwellings. A fire warden had been appointed by the Common Council in March, but he was extremely lax in enforcing fire regulations in the business section of the town.

The Council was no more effective in dealing with the problem of what the local newspaper described as the "frail fair ones." A petition to remove them all to a single assigned street was presented to the Council, but serious objections were voiced because of the possibility of litigation and the "useless expense, which in our infant state we are now unable to bear."[7]

The town's police force patrolled the streets, but it was hardly overzealous in the performance of its duties. One officer, when informed that a pickpocket was loitering nearby, replied: "Let the poor devil alone; there is nothing here to steal, and he will soon be starved out." The officers were pressed hard to control "drunken brawls and bloody fights," and they made short shrift of drunks. One man, who lay inebriated in the streets, was unceremoniously carted off to the station house where he was fined one dollar. Unapprehended also were the bands of thieves who were carrying off unguarded, stray stock in and around Austin. The prevailing suspicion was that people belonging to parties outfitting for the spring exodus to other mining fields were to blame. Fortunately, the difficulties of life in Austin were not compounded by a reign of homicidal terror during the winter months. Clubbings were the closest the town came to violence of this sort.[8]

The depressed business conditions of the winter of 1864-65 were responsible for some of the public's apathy. The payment of taxes on assessed valuation of property in the county, which should have brought in $54,450.53, was universally evaded. The assessor showed only a meager net collection of $4,000 by January, 1865. The lack of money for public expenditure was not the exclusive cause of ineffective government; public neglect of other community obligations probably undermined the morale of elected officials. But in spite of many lapses, the Common Council did provide eventually for a sewer and conduit through the town's main thoroughfare and constructed a jail and a city hall.[9]

Despite problems in government, concrete signs of progress were reported eagerly by the community builders. Some of the advances were humble enough, but in a new country where the inhabitants were far from home and friends, even the rudiments of civilized life made a powerful impression. The People's Restaurant, where three meals a day cost $1.50 and board for the week was $10, was recommended for its excellent fare. A more ample supply of water for the town, soon to be made available with the completion of a tunnel financed by the proprietors of the city reservoir, was eagerly awaited. The town boasted of having the best-stocked drugstore in the Territory; and the construction of many new buildings, some of them quite substantial brick edifices, gave an aura of permanence to the place.

The sense of community was evident in the agitation, in the autumn of 1864, to erect a public school building. The matter was formally discussed in late October, and supporters of a public school (a private school for boys and girls was available) contended that more money was squandered in Austin in one day than was needed to support a school for three months. Soon, a district school was opened, equipped with an excellent stove that afforded warmth to thirty-nine scholars. The number of pupils was to double within a fifteen-month period, but the majority of school-age children were nevertheless not enrolled, possibly because of the small tuition required.[10]

By 1865, the town had five clergymen, twelve physicians, and thirty-three lawyers, whose presence provided additional evidence of civilization. Samuel Bowles, who visited Austin in 1865, found the advantages of urban life in "the best French restaurant I have met since New York, a daily newspaper," and the luxury of the "boot-blacks and barbers and baths."[11]

Main Street afforded excitement and danger, and accidents were not infrequent. A few days after the Gallys arrived, a two-horse team broke away from its driver, headed down the street toward the Wells, Fargo & Company office, and tore off the awning in front of the building. Wagons loaded with every conceivable kind of merchandise rumbled into Austin: four hundred dozen eggs from Salt Lake City; wood cut in the nearby hills and selling for $6 per cord; tomatoes, corn, cabbage, potatoes, and onions from the Reese River area; grapes, apples, and provisions from California by fast freight; flour from Carson City; four thousand letters from the East by the Overland Stage; and barley and vegetables from Salt Lake.

Hundreds of different faces, some known and some unknown, appeared on Main Street each day. Emigrant wagons from Iowa, Idaho, Missouri, and Colorado pulled wearily up to the summit, with their horses, mules, and oxen in ragged condition. Some celebrated personalities of the day came through on stage. William M. Stewart and William H. Claggett, Nevada lawyers, both came to campaign; Ross Browne, the publicist and mineral resources expert, passed through on his way to Salt Lake City. The *Reveille* declared: "We trust he will return single, if not blessed."[12]

For Mat Gally, impressions of the area were formed over a period of several months. Since the Gallys were living in a warehouse in Clifton, the entrance to the two-mile-long canyon and the sights it offered were familiar to her. She could look out her door on any day of the week to see wagons, coaches, and strings of oxen entering and leaving the canyon. She brushed shoulders in Clifton with all types of people from all classes and every part of the world. The extraordinary social and political freedom of the community was a matter of wonder to her. There was fascination in this fast-moving, bustling world:

> The country is new & the population heterogeneous—you
> see every grade of every nationality
> represented—Americans from everywhere that have been
> everywhere—elderly portly capitalists that are here to
> invest—keen elegant speculators that have been
> successful—hairy, hungry "hard" looking miners, some

that have "struck it" & some that haven't. Mill-owners
& mill hands—merchants, doctors, lawyers, sailors,
saddlers, "butcher & baker" every thing and
everybody—riches & rags—broadcloths &
fustians—"greasers" with their black faces & slouched
hats, "Castilians" with their fierce moustachios &
jingling spurs—Frenchman, Englishmen, Prussians
Russians Poles Swiss Dutch Jews Irishmen &
Scots—Indians with their blankets & half naked squaws
with their papooses bound to a board, hanging down their
back from a band that passes round their [the squaws']
head. You can live as you please, dress as you please,
eat as you please, make money as you please, or lose it
as you please, go where & as you please & die & be
burried or not as you please. One man hurrahs for Abe &
his neighbor for Jeff—one man drinks to the health of the
Repubs or "Blks" as they call them here & another gives
as his toast "Davis & his cabinet" or "Lee & his
Gents." In the street you hear every tongue and language
from the grunt of the Shoshones to the soft music of the
Italian—see every costume coats cloaks shawls wraps
poncho serapes & blankets—great long droves of pack
mules, driven usually by Mexicans with their little ponies
& queer whips, passing some great towering wood or
lumber wagon holding two or three cords of wood &
hauled by their overworked oxen which require the most
peculiar & extensive profanity that ever you heard to get
them along—along will come the coach with its
thoroughly groomed & well fed horses dashing through
the narrow street—perhaps running into a drove of
camels with their long beards and ugly necks at which
sight the horses most decidely "shy" & no wonder. You
see great big freight wagons from California or Salt Lake,
bigger than the old National Road wagon drawn by
sometimes 10 & sometimes 20 mules all driven by a
single line. Everybody, women as well as men ride at full
galop up hill and down—almost everybody gambles,
play faro, monte rondeaux or billiards checkers chess &
dominoes—women usually Spanish or French hire tables

in the different saloons & play all night. The Chinamen
with their loose shirts, long queues & wooden shoes do
nearly all of the washing.[13]

The great freedom of life in Austin also was evident
in political life. During a period of fierce sectional
division and in the midst of a bloody civil war, politics
was freely discussed. This had been unthinkable in Ohio,
where political passions had attained new levels of
violence after the Gallys left. Mat wrote to her father that
"we have not lived politically so freely for years." When
Richmond fell, followed by Lee's surrender, many
people, according to Mat, "expressed their sorrow
openly,"[14] and the excitement that prevailed when news
was flashed of Lincoln's assassination was intense. For
the last year of the war, the Gallys found in Nevada the
freedom from civil passion they had dreamed of in Ohio.

But the Gallys now faced not political but personal
problems. Mat put on a good face about the trials of living
in a warehouse, and she found that there were positive
benefits to residing in Clifton: it had more light, warmth,
and pleasantness than the main business district farther up
the canyon. The real problem was making it through the
winter without totally depleting their resources. Prices
were comparatively high, with one-room houses renting
for $20 per month and provisions costing a family of four
from $15 to $20 per month. Daily wages fluctuated
between $4 to $5 for common laborers and $6 for
mechanics. Professional men set their own prices, with
doctors charging between $5 and $50 per visit and lawyers
waxing rich on suits and countersuits over mining claims
and other litigation. "If you have money," observed Mat,
"you can live very comfortably if you are poor it is hard

here as it is every place I ever saw. You pay coin & take coin. You can buy nothing for less than a 'bit' 10 cts or 12½ indiscriminately; no smaller coin being in circulation.''[15]

Loud talk of new strikes, fortunes being made and lost, and bold plans and vast hopes abounded at Reese River. The exhilarating autumn days and the bustling adventurousness of the people opened vistas of success, and the doctor was caught up in the prevailing mood of optimism. He went to the Recorder's Office to examine deeds to mining properties and came away impressed by the paper valuations: revenue stamps bought in a single day covered $800,000 in transactions.[16] Dr. Gally had discovered two silver mines,[17] but by late fall the Reese River Mining District entered a period of borrasca (meaning that good-working ore was not being extracted), and he did not strike a rich vein of ore.

Exercising caution, Dr. Gally turned to means of support other than mining. Politics brought him in contact with a number of prominent Democratic lawyers and politicians, and almost as soon as he had arrived in Austin, he was drafted into the political campaign of 1864. He worked on behalf of the former congressional territorial delegate from Nevada, A. C. Bradford, a brother-in-law of General Halleck. Bradford ran for a congressional seat in the November election but was defeated and immediately afterwards turned to a get-rich-quick scheme. The subject of his rosy optimism was valuable agricultural lands along the projected route of the Central Pacific Railroad. All he and the men who joined his company had to do was journey a hundred miles in search of these lands, located in the desolate country where the headwaters of the Humboldt River rise. Dr.

Gally knew nothing about mines, but he knew good farming land; rather than see his greenbacks decrease in value, he decided to stake his money on this plan as everyone else was doing.

After spending two months in Nevada, the doctor was to leave on December 2 with the other members of the company for the headwaters of the Humboldt River. He planned to be away about ten days. Up until the time of his departure, Mat and the children were in comparatively good health, although to the discerning eye, Mat was suffering from physical and emotional strain. She was much more worn out from the overland journey than the doctor cared to admit to others. Her energies were drained; the "terror and excitement" of the Indians, "shame and anxiety" about Fuller, and the final abdication of responsibility for her brother had brought her to the breaking point. She worried about Fuller's whereabouts. Her sense of isolation was deepened by the lack of mail from home. Each day's visit to the post office turned up nothing, and letters of inquiry to the post office in San Francisco yielded nothing.

Then, too, the weather took a foreboding turn before the doctor's departure. Autumn was drawing to a close, and winter was in the air. During the early days of November, snow had fallen and the nights had turned very cold. Somewhat deceptively, the sun melted the snow and the days became clear and warm again, but by the second week of the month, a wet snow fell and was followed by cooler, clear days. Soon a white mantle of snow, accompanied by sub-zero temperatures, would cover the ground. On November 28, a Monday, the snow began to fall and "the surrounding hills looked as cold and bleak as a Norwegian's hell."[18] By Thursday evening, the temperature had fallen below zero and the old-timers thought that night was the coldest in two years. On the following morning, Dr. Gally departed.

The trip the doctor had begun deepened Mat's anxieties. She had no one to depend upon but her husband, and the obvious dangers posed by the weather and a possible mishap made the idea of separation almost unbearable to her. At any rate, no sooner had the Doctor departed than all of her anxieties precipitated a "low nervous fever." She was on her own, with the care and safety of the children uppermost in her mind, but she could not rally her flagging energies and collapsed. For the next eighteen days, she "never expected & hardly hoped to see another new year."

The neighbors knew of her pitiful plight and did everything they could for her. They summoned Dr. Murphy, who had practiced medicine for fourteen years in San Francisco and before that in New York City. Dr. Murphy watched over her and encouraged her with "excessive kindness and patience," and the neighbors did the same. Months later, in a letter to her father, Mat recalled with gratitude the helpfulness of these people:

> I never recd from my own friends more kindness than I
> have from people here—have never known more
> agreeable scholarly men. I do wish all of you were not so
> far off—however great the kindness of friends they are
> not your own kith. I never saw a people so patient &
> uncomplaining in want & misery or so prodigal in
> plenty.[19]

While Mat was confined to her bed, the first real snows of winter ushered in the holiday season. The ragamuffins pelted each other and passersby with snowballs. Sleighs appeared, and a gay, festive mood prevailed everywhere. Austin's clubs planned social evenings: the "Merry Bachelors" had their sociable the opening week of December, followed the next day by a ball at the Nevada Hotel in upper Austin, where food and wine were plentiful and the waltz and quadrille were danced.

Mat expected Dr. Gally to return by December 12, but he did not appear, and a fresh snow fell on the following day. By the middle of the week, everyone was talking about the worst blizzard since November 1, 1863. All traffic had stopped, the freighters were not rolling over the roads, and a general lethargy settled over the Reese River community. Snow began to fall again on Friday night, throwing up high drifts. Word filtered into Austin that the Indians in the surrounding country lacked food and were slaughtering cattle whenever they found any. By the end of the week, the temperature had fallen below freezing and the cold was bitter; in fact, the weather was the worst that anyone could remember in the short history of the settlement. New reports circulated about the numbers of frozen cattle that had been sighted.

Some of the gloom dissipated for a few hours on Monday evening as parties of pretty women and gay young men took to their sleighs, breaking the stillness with the "ringing of bells and the crackling of crisp snow." Tuesday, however, brought more cold and new reports about the terrible effects of the freezing temperatures. A man who lived in a cabin on the Overland Road, about forty-eight miles west of Austin, encountered two huge gray wolves who had pursued a horse to his door. There were a number of teamsters who had their feet frozen or who had suffered other forms of frostbite that resulted in amputation.

Gaiety still prevailed among sleighing enthusiasts. Sleigh rides down the steep hills occupied the young and even the members of the Common Council, who abandoned civic responsibility for sport. Bobsleds shot down the hills at fantastic speeds, one hurtling past a street lounger at what seemed to be ninety miles an hour. The hardier men and boys did capers on sleds descending from the canyon hills, arising from the ground at the end of the course with rent pants.[20]

The cold began to ease off by the middle of the week. For days, Mat believed she would never see her husband again, but on Thursday, December 22, the party of bedraggled men arrived in Austin, having "lost their way, nearly frozen & half starved." Dr. Gally came home to learn that his wife had come as close to losing her life as he had his.

The five men in the party had tramped through the snow toward the rough country south and east of present-day Elko. Caught in a violent mid-December blizzard, they found a crude shelter in which to wait out the storm. Supplies began to run out and they faced actual starvation. The feeling of isolation and impending doom was embedded in Dr. Gally's memory:

> ... ghostly in the sleeting winter snows under the moon and stars, when the silence of Nature is more still in this inanimate land than the white tombs silvered by the moon in the country graveyard, near a deserted village in the black track where pestilential war has strewn with broken guns the ruined fields, and crushed, in his barbaric grasp, the humble throb of industry and thrift, that he may write with undisturbed display his name in blood—and read it—D-e-s-o-l-a-t-i-o-n.[21]

After a trek of 120 miles, the party surveyed 5,000

acres of land and located a number of silver ledges. Whatever the agricultural value of the land due to the presence of water and the proximity of the Central Pacific tracks, there was no ready market for farm products. Like hundreds of Nevada ventures, the South Humboldt River speculation had little more to recommend it than the claims of its promoters.[22] The scheme foundered when A. C. Bradford, who had originally advocated the idea, was entrusted to sell the properties on the New York market. In time, the hapless speculators learned that Bradford had not received the necessary survey papers and titles from Nevada and had dropped the entire matter.

Dr. Gally was slow to realize the worthlessness of his first Nevada business speculation. In a letter to his father-in-law, written toward the end of January, he minimized the expense, enlarged the chances of success, and iterated his great faith in the country. As for the well-being of his own family, all was well there, too. The children were in excellent health, and Mat was "very well" after her illness. Dr. Gally had no worries about Fuller either, for he had been in good health when he left them and business conditions in California, where he supposedly had gone, were apparently improving.[23] At this time and for years to come, he closed his eyes to the heavy sacrifices frontier life demanded of his family.

The year 1864 ended on a quiet note for the Gallys. The family spent Christmas Eve and Day together, turning down an invitation to dine out. The town itself was in high holiday spirits, and the weather had improved. On Christmas Day, several fights broke out in the crowded streets and a brawl occurred at the Log Cabin Saloon. The worst incident, however, took place in a bawdy house: the courtesans had staged a dance, which came abruptly to an end when a bystander slapped the faces of a dancing couple, following it up with two shots from a derringer. One of the bullets lodged in the male dancer's leg, and the injury nearly claimed his life. With holiday spirits played out, a deep calm and tranquillity descended upon Reese River.[24]

4

Great Expectations

THE WINTER of 1864-65 was difficult for everyone at Reese River. Years later, the doctor remembered clearly the bleak outlook: "The fall of 1864 was a very hard one for miners in Reese River; no money, no work, flour twenty-five gold dollars per cwt., and other things in proportion."[1] In January, the leading mining companies threatened a wage reduction. Many miners complained that they were not receiving their wages, or at best were being paid in greenbacks. The local courts were besieged by anxious miners filing suits to wring their wages from men who were financially bankrupt, and the *Reveille* of January 27, 1865, called down upon the miscreant mine owners the "curse of God," promising "to warn the public against these law-abiding thieves."

By the end of January, there were reports of families who were without the necessities of life, and the sufferings of these people were heightened by heavy snows and the bitterly cold weather that followed. The city government, aided by civic-minded individuals, met the emergency by raising a relief fund for those families who had nothing, a fund which tided them over until spring. Single men had to seek help from less indigent friends.[2]

Bad times at Reese River were followed by the slowing of business activity on the Pacific slope and by the ugly prospect of the collapse of the Reese River mining boom. Mines that had produced rich chloride ore to a depth of sixty or seventy feet were yielding barren rock, and consternation was reflected on many faces. A new search for paying ore at lower depths was expected to begin in the spring, and the future of the district depended upon the success or failure of these probes.[3]

Uneasiness about the future was not allayed by the fierce winter weather. A letup in the bitter cold came toward the end of January, and the appearance of the sun and the warmer temperatures prompted the *Reveille* to expostulate that ''we can almost imagine that the gentle winds bear on their wings from far off sunny climes, the fragrant breath of the magnolia, the orange and the peach bloom.'' The snow, however, was piled in six-foot drifts on the summit above Telegraph Canyon, and the reprieve from bad weather was a short one.

By the middle of February, a new storm laid a fresh blanket of snow, ''rendering still more bleak and desolate this always dreary spot.''[4] The winter cold extended into March, and snowdrifts in mid-March were still covering the mouths of shafts and making the mountains impassable. Herds of antelope and mountain sheep had been forced down from the high slopes into the low-lying hills. The sufferings of the Indians had begun with the first bad snows in December, and reports of their continued plight made sad reading. Toward the end of February, an Indian was discovered dead—huddled over a burned out campfire—in the Cortez District. The destitution of the Indians would put them on the warpath in the spring.

Despite personal and community tribulations, there was a lighter side to life at Reese River. The mining district's newspaper tried to raise a laugh when it could. One romantic farce featured a Reese River miner and his new bride. Their troubles began when they took in a few boarders, with whom the bride was extremely popular. The bridegroom became intensely jealous and suspicious, and induced a bosom friend to test his wife's fidelity. The Iago pursued her and fell in love with her, but she kept her peace until he announced his intentions. She barely heard him to the end before she treated his head to the poker tongs, and when her husband entered the room and tried to intercede for his friend, she gave him some of the same. She then packed her belongings and left the house.[5]

Other light puffs were printed occasionally to maintain Austin's reputation for lightheartedness. A rash of fights and other diverting incidents in March kept the Recorder's Office busy and were covered in the newspaper. In a satirical manner, the *Reveille* reported that two women were brawling in the Recorder's Office, "which resulted in one fainting and the other having a miscarriage." The victorious combatant of another fight was summoned to appear before the Recorder. The Judge fined him $5, whereupon "the gentleman 'saw' the Judge and went him fifteen better for costs. The vanquished one then sued for damages or repairs, we don't know which, but failed to 'make the riffle.'"[6]

Other types of popular entertainment were available during the winter months. Austinites flocked to the theatre, no matter what play was presented. The presentation of ``The Enraged Politician and the Lottery Ticket`` packed Bradford's Hall on a Saturday evening in February, even though the play was performed without benefit of scenery. Another play, ``Black-Eyed Susan,`` scheduled for February 22, had to be called off when one of the actors began cutting bacchanalian capers. Carrie Chapman, dancer and actress, captivated an audience with her performance. Occasional balls and concerts were held at Bradford's Hall, one of them sponsored by the Hook and Ladder Company.

During the bleak winter months, when Austin's future seemed uncertain, the best element in the community turned to constructive endeavors. At the beginning of February, there was talk of establishing a public library financed by money raised from a lecture series. The *Reveille* took up the idea and reported that a businessman had promised a $500 subscription in the event plans were worked out. Nothing came of the project in the following months; money was needed more urgently for relief purposes. A special charity night, netting $300, was held in March at Bradford's Hall. In lieu of a public library, some of the better-run saloons provided a reading room offering a variety of newspaper and periodical literature.[7]

The ingrained optimism of the people would not be stifled. Many looked to the spring for a new surge of prosperity. Talk ran high of the Eastern money on its way, of the new mills under construction, and of the emigrant parties ready to start from the Mississippi states. But for all the talk about the good days to come, the spring months brought bad news and tragedy. The *Reveille* announced Lincoln's assassination in its April 15 issue and reported the intense feeling of loss that, with the exception of a few men who had made incautious remarks for which they were chastised, was felt everywhere. The town's officers were encouraged to bring in any person "expressing joy." The *Reveille* urged vehemently that the culprits "must be hunted and punished to the extent of the law." Mat's comments to her father reflected the typical response from Democrats in 1865. She wrote that "we recd news of the tragedy at Washington about 10 o'clk A.M. Sat 15th—it created a great excitement among the people—but those who live by the sword must perish by the sword & I hope we may all gather as we sow."[8]

Much closer to home, the beginning of April brought reports of an Indian raid on a herd of cattle grazing forty-five miles northwest of Austin in the vicinity of Fish Creek. The band of Paiutes wounded one man and killed a boy, whose body was abandoned after the scalp had been taken. This incident was followed by a series of raids north of the Humboldt River in Paradise Valley, where scattered attacks on prospectors resulted in the death of three white men in March.

Ranches and isolated settlements in the valley were particularly subject to Indian attacks. A number of families, fleeing their homes in the valley, were trapped in a corral by a war party, and a massacre was narrowly averted when one of the men successfully rode through the Indian lines to summon help. Two men occupying a cabin did not leave the area soon enough and were cut down by the bullets of the Indians as they fled their burning cabin. By mid-April, regular army troops supported by citizens were scouring the country. They surprised Indians near Kane Spring and took eighteen scalps.

The uprising in northern Humboldt County of the Paiutes, led by Black Rock Tom and the Shoshones and Bannocks he had recruited for his war parties, worked up the Shoshone tribe in Lander County. The Shoshone, who had been dominated by the Paiutes before the Reese River mining boom of 1862-63, had been considered dependable by the white men. The month of May brought shocked surprise as reports of Shoshone raids in the county increased. The raids on livestock quartered in the vicinity of Austin were attributed to the Indians in the valleys east of Austin and their shiftless white friends.

The excitement in Austin was intense, and early in May forty men joined a company of Reese River volunteers to await the arrival of regular troops from Fort Ruby before beginning a thirty-day campaign. The tenseness in Austin was aggravated both by a report that 500 Indians were holding talks in Monitor Valley and by a communication from Major McDermitt to E. C. Brearley that the Indians could be expected to move against Austin and Star City.

Help was on the way, however. Lieutenant Seamonds came in from Fort Ruby with scouts and an Indian interpreter and announced that the main force soon would arrive. He picked up the trail of a band of sixty Indians whom he tracked into the mountains west of Austin, engaged in combat, and defeated. There were no casualties among Seamonds' forces.

The possibility of an Indian assault against any of the Reese River settlements faded after the vanquished band fled to northern Nevada, although hostilities there continued through the remaining months of 1865. The terrible predicament of many of the tribes was seen by Governor H. G. Blasdel in personal meetings with the

Indians: they were without food and blamed their troubles on the white man. The Governor admitted frankly that he could offer them little hope and even less help.[9]

The rigors of pioneering were soon balanced by large doses of new activity and hope. During the winter of 1865, people like the Gallys struggled to hold on, and by the spring of 1865, a new wave of speculation hit Reese River. The search for metal-bearing ore at lower depths began with the arrival of money from Eastern promoters. Under the stimulus of new investment capital, all branches of business benefited. Goods, machinery, and lumber were hauled in, bringing estimated freight costs for 1865 to $1,381,800. Wells, Fargo & Company covered the cost of these and other imports by handling $6,000,000 in bullion.

Vigorous exploration in the second half of 1865 disclosed good-paying sulphuret ores below the 80-foot level and in some mines at the 300-foot level. The discovery of rich sulphurets at lower depths restored confidence in the mines. An old difficulty, however, would continue to plague the district in the years ahead. The refractory ores, which were reduced by the roasting process first employed by Vanderbosch, added to milling costs. As a result, the mining ventures in this district had to depend on speculation to make money.[10]

As the long winter finally drew to an end, the Gallys could look again to the future. Mat's spirits were lifted by the first letters from home in a year; they were from her father and sister Rebec. She had almost given up hope of hearing again from them, and the excitement she felt upon receiving these letters was overwhelming. "To say I was glad, is to say nothing—I was so excited & weak," she wrote, "that I laid down the remainder of the day—to think of a whole year passing and I not knowing whether you were alive or dead!'' She had thought of them all, often and long. Her stepmother and father were living in the big, old house alone. She was not surprised about Rebec's marriage to Captain Cunningham, and, of course, she hoped ''she will never regret it.'' Her brother, George, was a lawyer in Boston, married, and well-off, and she was happy for him. There was comfort, too, in thinking that her younger sister, Hattie, was enjoying George's hospitality.

One matter alone deeply disturbed her: she had to account for Fuller to her father. She wrote: ''First, about Fuller, we do not know at all where he is—have no idea excepting that he said he was going to Sacramento—and talked sometimes of going down to the coast and getting aboard a vessel. All of our efforts to hear from him have been in vain.'' She did not mention that the doctor's speculation had consumed their savings and that Fuller's money had been invested in the same way as theirs.[11] Inevitably, a rift between father and daughter developed over Fuller, but more than two years elapsed before this came about.

As heavy as some of her burdens were, Mat took comfort in the knowledge that the three she loved were thriving. ''The Doctor's health,'' she wrote her father, ''is very good & the children stronger than ever they were—Jimmy particularly, improves—has had no diarrhea for a year—I don't think you would know him he has grown so much & is so browned & roughened—yesterday he wore his first 'suspender trousers' & jacket & he feels 'big.' The children neither of them have extended their book knowledge, but still are not behind many of their age.''[12] With the welfare of her brood to consider, she understood that her own personal misgivings and heartache had to be repressed, and the best way to do it was by useful employment. In the same letter to her father, she declared: "I do my own work & am very busy—you know I always was busy & I have not lost the faculty." She did admit, however, that her hair had turned gray and she felt like an "old woman."

* * *

The winter that had been spent awaiting developments, exploring mining opportunities, and prospecting slipped away. The doctor's speculation had consumed their savings, making further mining investments impossible at this time. Their illusions about the South Humboldt River property, however, had not entirely been destroyed. "The land," declared Mat, "was, is & must even be valuable for its water, timber, grass climate fish & soil but the difficulty lay in holding it without actual possession." [13]

The valley where the land and mines were located was too isolated for actual settlement. The Gallys had to do something practical to make money, for during the winter, money had been going out but not coming in. The doctor's prospecting at Reese River had not produced much income, either.

The Gallys had looked carefully at the agricultural potential of the land and realized that the sagebrush soil was extremely fertile; Mat praised the quality of the beets, cabbage, potatoes, turnips, carrots, and parsnips grown in the Reese River area, as well as the wild berries of superior taste which were found growing profusely near the river's source. Dairy farming seemed to hold the most promise, and the Gallys considered this possibility seriously. Milk, butter, eggs, and chickens were selling at good prices, and even during the summer months butter was not plentiful and had to be imported. As tempting as the idea was for the Gallys, it had to be abandoned. They did not have the money to invest in cows and poultry. Without sufficient money or means, they decided to give hay farming a try and the doctor busied himself looking for ranchland[14] (which, under the Homestead Act of 1862, was available free to settlers).

About seventy miles east of Austin on the Overland Mail Road, Dr. Gally found land that looked good for a hay ranch. The land was located about four miles up Roberts Canyon on the western slope of the Roberts Creek Mountains in the territory of the Shoshone. The ride up the canyon could not be equalled for beauty anywhere along the Overland Road. "Wild flowers of new varieties and great beauty carpet the ground," wrote one traveler, "while cedar trees afford a grateful shade from an oppressive sun."[15] Some miles east was the Diamond Mountain Mining District, which had been organized in June of the previous year and had shown indications of mineral veins extending several miles along the western flank of the mountain.

The ranch had some speculative value and was closer to the South Humboldt River lands than was Austin. Thus, traffic coming over the road in opposite directions from Austin and Salt Lake could stop there. The White Pine mines to the north appeared on the verge of a major boom, but this did not materialize for another two years. Plentiful grass, wood, and water made the area extremely suitable for stock ranching, factors that attracted the Gallys to Roberts Creek.

Sometime before the end of the summer, and possibly as early as the spring, the Gallys moved to Roberts Creek and pitched their tent. The energy of the country was in the doctor's blood. He saw the Overland Road settled with more people and houses; he had seen the "elephant": "Everything in this country goes by jumps—there is no crawling—no standing still—cities of half the size and quite as fine as Zanesville are built in three years and moved off elsewhere in two other years." Almost accidentally, he had fallen into the business habits of the Nevada frontier. A man had to look forward, venture more than a little, hope for success, and be prepared for reverses. He stated this prevailing philosophy succinctly when he explained to his father-in-law the reasons for his optimism: "I have endeavored to see the value of this place, in futuro, if I am not mistaken it will be well done—but if I am mistaken it will not be quite so well."[16] Nor was Dr. Gally alone in attaching great value to the ranch. A former member of the Austin bar, Henry J. Labatt, passed over the Overland Road with his family on the way to the Eastern states and was enthusiastic about the potential future of the region. He believed that the ranch would be the site of another Austin as the mining districts in the vicinity came into their own.

The doctor had formed a partnership with at least one other man in the Roberts Creek venture and probably had arranged with two others to work the hay on shares. The ranch was referred to as "Gauley and Parkins." Three men—Parker, Tom, and Bell—shared the work around the place with the doctor. The Gallys had brought to the ranch all their belongings, which included seven horses, three wagons, five chickens, one cow, two dogs, and by the beginning of February, twelve oxen. As a temporary expedient, the ranchers sold hay at $.03 to $.05 per pound to the overland travelers and teamsters.

Roberts Creek was a delightful place in which to live during the spring and summer months, and camping out there in a tent was not a hardship until the cold weather set in. Life was quiet there. Freighters and coaches lumbered by, and men on foot came along frequently. These travelers were the Gallys' only contacts with the outer world.

In both June and July, there was trouble along the Overland Road to the east of Roberts Creek. In June, two young California men brutally murdered three men near Schell Creek Station who were returning to their homes in Iowa with a band of half-breed horses. The perpetrators of the horrible crime were arrested; Ransom Young was held in Egan by Justice Murphy, and John Wab was in the hands of the justice of the peace at Camp Crittenden. A mob took the men from the authorities, treating them to death by hanging. A month later, a man named Henry Wonder murdered his partner, Henry Baker, several miles west of Egan Canyon. After wandering around in the sagebrush country for four days, Wonder came back to the stage road looking for food. He fell in with some teamsters who delivered him to the justice of the peace at Egan Canyon. A mob tried unsuccessfully to lynch Wonder, but the rope they were using broke. Disgusted with their half-botched efforts, they returned Wonder to the justice of the peace. In a jury trial in September, he was acquitted for lack of evidence.[17] In spite of the unsettled state of the area, the peace and quiet at the ranch was not disturbed.

Toward the end of the summer, the doctor felt free enough from his ranching responsibilities to go to Austin to run for public office. The Democrats had nominated him for a seat in the state assembly, believing he would attract the newly arrived emigrant voter, and he actively campaigned in Austin during the last week of October.

The Democratic meeting on the evening of October 27 was held outside the saloon of John Grimes (who would kill Stephen Lynnis, known as the "Dublin Chicken," three weeks later in a post-election quarrel). H. K. Mitchell, the Democratic candidate for Congress, Judge Reed, and Dr. Gally sat on the platform. The audience, warmed by a roaring bonfire, listened to the orators. Mitchell raved about the possibility of Sambo and Pompey taking the seats of Clay, Webster, and Douglas in the Senate, and he concluded his speech by declaiming hysterically that the wives and daughters of white men would be forced to sup with Negroes. "To come nearer home," the *Reveille* of October 27 reported, "he even thought it possible that a Congo law-giver might warm the seat of our present District Judge." Comments of this kind, in a Republican stronghold, were self-defeating and ludicrous. When Dr. Gally's turn came to speak, he kept his sense of humor, treated the audience to liberal doses of his wit, and made the meeting, in the phrase of one bystander, "as good as a circus."[18] On Election Day, November 7, however, both Mitchell and the doctor were defeated, and the doctor returned to his prospects at Roberts Creek.

Work at the ranch proceeded in spurts. During the late summer, the men stacked the hay in the fields. Work on the stockade house proceeded slowly, however, and not until the beginning of January was it nearing completion. In the final stages, Mr. Tom worked on the roof for a couple of hours one day, and Mr. Parker helped a few days later when he felt well enough to get up from a sickbed. After returning from a week's trip to Austin, the doctor pitched in and had the room daubed, the roof ready for a covering of earth, and the dirt floor thawed. Their new house was primitive, but was ready for habitation by the second week in January. Once the outside was completed, the men built a cupboard, shelves, a table, and chairs. On cold winter nights, Dr. Gally mended the harness, and both he and Mr. Tom built a snowsled for the children. Mat baked, ironed, sewed, and wrote letters.

Although the Gallys busied themselves as much as they could, the winter at Roberts Creek meant for Mat the most complete isolation she had ever experienced. The Christmas of 1865 came and went with the Gallys remaining almost completely unaware of the holiday season. The doctor or his associates were always around, but the weather kept Mat inside the gloomy cabin for months at a time. The cold and snow persisted through the winter months into late spring. When it was not snowing, the wind was blowing. Only occasionally was the sky clear and blue ''as ever Italy saw & as unclouded.''[19] The nights were terribly cold. Toward the end of January, the water in the cabin froze. At night, Mat would peer out the cabin door to see if a south wind was bringing snow and rain, and the wind whistling over the valley floor left her in the doldrums.

Activities from day to day did not vary greatly. As weather permitted, Bell or Parker hauled firewood from the nearby wooded slopes or spent time rounding up the horses, routine jobs that kept them barely busy. An impetus to activity came toward the end of January when the doctor signed a contract to supply logs to a business party in Austin. He left the ranch for Austin on January 21 to buy the oxen for the heavy work ahead. Thirteen days later, he had returned with ten oxen and a wagon.

The logs were to come from the White Pine country. Reports from the White Pine district, organized during the previous autumn, indicated that there were large forests of nut pine and cedar in the foothills, and at higher elevations were the most extensive tree growths to be found anywhere in the Great Basin. The major handicaps to the doctor's plans were the cold weather and the unexplored nature of the country. He and his partners would practically be trailblazing their own road from the Overland Road to White Pine, a distance of about fifty miles.[20]

Traveling over the sagebrush country in winter was a hazardous business, as Dr. Gally knew from previous experience. Late in January the Gallys saw two men who barely had survived an encounter with the elements. They had both come from the White Pine country; one of them was suffering from snow blindness and the other had his "big toe frozen black." The man with the frozen toes, John Beard of Zanesville, had been caught in a snowstorm and had unfortunately wet his lucifer matches, an accident which was the beginning of his troubles. When Beard reached the Overland Road at Ruby, Dr. Long amputated the middle finger of his left hand and put him on the stage for Austin, where Dr. Morton and Dr. Chamblin removed the toes and other gangrened areas of one foot.[21]

While Dr. Gally and Bell were marking out a road toward the White Pine country, Mat was justifiably worried. "I am," she noted when they did not return within six days, "very anxious about the Dr & if he does not come by tomorrow night shall be alarmed."[22] The two men returned weary and with their rations depleted, but they had marked out a wagon road to the White Pine Range. In later years, their route would provide major access to White Pine from the Central Pacific railhead at Palisade.

A last effort to obtain the logs came in mid-February. Bell and Parker were away twelve days, spending nearly nine days covering fifty to sixty miles. They struggled through snowdrifts twelve to fifteen feet deep and had to abandon some of the oxen and the wagon. The snowdrifts and the cold were too much for them.

Having encountered too many obstacles, the doctor abandoned the logging enterprise. At the beginning of the third week in April, he drove the cattle back to Austin. During his absence, Mat felt a deepening gloom. The days were cold and windy, and each new day seemed more dreary than the one before. In her diary for April 28, she wrote: "No letter, no Dr, no horses or wagons, no anything today but whirlwinds." Hard luck cases drifted along the road. A man with two small boys stopped at the ranch. His horses had been stolen, and the family was making its way on foot through the snow-covered valley.

The first week of May, the doctor finally arrived home with new plans. He was ready to try something different, and he seized eagerly the suggestion by his political cronies in Austin that he run again on the Democratic ticket for a seat in the state legislature. Although not abdicating his interest in the Roberts Creek ranch (Mr. Tom was to stay on), the doctor realized that his ranching venture had not been particularly successful.

The rise to prominence of this part of Nevada was still in the future. The White Pine district had attracted some interest among miners by February 1866, but the ore extracted was of low grade. Not until 1868 did Treasure Hill ore set off the White Pine mining boom. Discoveries were made in New York Canyon as early as 1864, and the Eureka district (which was not too many miles south of Roberts Creek) was organized. But the absence of capital and later the inability to reduce the ores satisfactorily delayed the real opening of the district. The doctor was not wrong about the future of the region, but success was a matter of timing.[23]

Mat did not regret leaving Roberts Creek for Austin after the isolation and hardships of the winter. With a feeling of relief, she packed their belongings and loaded the wagon on May 13. She gave the children permission to sleep that night in the wagon. One last mishap occurred on Sunday evening when the doctor injured his knee with a pitchfork. On the following morning, they started despite the injury, with the doctor lying in the wagon resting his hurt knee. Mat drove the team while the children, for most of the day, rode the horses.

The family pitched its tent the first night out in a sagebrush valley. On Tuesday, they climbed from the valley floor into the Toiyabe Range and reached the summit one mile above Austin, where they staked their camp for the night. The doctor went into Austin for beefsteak. While he was on the errand, the others collected sticks and brush for a fire. "Dr came with beef," Mat recorded, "and finally we had a good fire, good supper & good appetite."[24]

5

Fortune's Wheel

THE GALLYS left Roberts Creek in May of 1866 with nothing but the doctor's hopes to bolster them. Although he would keep busy tracking down every new prospecting and officeholding lead, he nevertheless had to earn a living. Seasonal work could be had harvesting hay on shares at one of the ranches near Austin, but real opportunities for regular employment were limited. Without the will to get away, the poverty of the independent poor man of Nevada was to be Dr. Gally's fate.

Mat realized by this time that fortune favored only the lucky few and that the Gallys did not belong to this class. She found it nearly impossible to accept their lot, but she could not bring herself to oppose her husband. As hard as life was, she remained silent in his presence, reserving her discontent for her diary. Frustrated by loneliness, insecurity, and hardships, she could only endure and hope. Had she been able to look into the future, the certain knowledge of the months and years of sacrifice and deprivation ahead would have chilled her heart. For the present, she struggled to meet the challenges of everyday living and to cheer herself with the thought that they were alive and well.

Thus far in pioneering, the Gallys had known only discomforts, and personal tragedy had not touched them. Other families in 1866 did not fare as well. One emigrant wagon, which passed the office of the *Reveille*, presented a pitiful sight: "A weary looking man sat on the seat driving the horses; a narrow bed laid on poles, and suspended from the frame holding the cover of the wagon, contained a sick woman, whose face was as pallid as death."[1] The nagging fear that they could easily be broken up as a family haunted Mat Gally.

The doctor was more optimistic than Mat and had all kinds of ideas for new ventures. The magnet was the region south and southeast of Reese River and a mine called the "Indian Jim," located in the Hot Creek Range 110 miles southeast of Austin. Austin, situated at the geographical center of the state, was an outfitting point for exploring expeditions in every direction. The mining districts in and around the town were staked out, and prospectors had to fan out for hundreds of miles in the hopes of making a new strike. In 1865, prospectors had penetrated south to the "Valley of Death" and the Amargosa, "the river of bitter waters."[2] Mat could have scant hope the doctor would remain quietly at Reese River for long, with mining boomlets in the Philadelphia, Morey, and Hot Creek mining districts.

In the meantime, the Reese River region offered one minor money-making opportunity during the latter part of the summer. There was abundant grass suitable for hay in

Gilson's Park, a few miles east of Austin in the vicinity of the Overland Road. About two-and-a-half weeks after their return, the family went out to look at the hay, but it would be more than a month before they moved to Gilson's ranch.

The main objective, however, was to resettle in Austin in advance of the fall elections. Rather than move into the town without immediate accommodations, the Gallys found on the eastern slope of the Toiyabe a deserted cabin with walls but no roof. They used the canvas from their tent for a roof, but the arrangement was hardly satisfactory. The weather remained unsettled in May. The wind blew fiercely on May 17, and Mat kept the children in the wagon during the worst of the gale. The next day was no better, and the gusts of wind unloosed the canvas cover. With the doctor more or less incapacitated as a result of his sore knee and a lame ankle incurred when a horse kicked him, Mat had to do the best she could.

The makeshift cabin continued to be a miserable affair. The wet snows that came during the last week of May made the situation extremely unpleasant; the canvas roof leaked water and the quarters were damp and cold. It was no small wonder that the Gallys were sick as the cold, windy, and wet weather extended into June. The doctor complained of neuralgia and the children of malaise.

Everyone had to remain as busy as possible to counteract the hard living conditions. The doctor made a point of going into Austin almost every day to stay abreast of developments, tend to business matters, shop, and find recreation in a barroom or at a horse race. On a few rare occasions, he condescended to take one or both of the children with him. Matty enjoyed one of these excursions immensely, eating the goodies that her father bought for her and watching attentively the passing throngs on the streets. Twice, the doctor took Jimmy with him, and on one of these trips the boy was thrilled to receive a small bound volume of Shakespeare from his father's friend, Mr. Pridham, a Wells, Fargo & Company employee. Mat was lonely waiting for the doctor to return, usually late in the day or at night, but she had to endure his absences along with the other hardships.

Mat's life was revolving more and more around Jimmy and Matty. Except for minor illnesses, they had grown stronger and more robust. Their formal educations had been neglected, but Mat spent much time tutoring them in fundamental skills and reading to them from the classics. Matty had become company for her mother during the doctor's frequent absences, and occasionally she helped out with the cleaning and washing. Jimmy did not have the endurance of his sister, was sick more often, and had a much more gentle disposition. Mat could see that he was a curious, observant boy who spent many of his hours watching men at work in a foundry or a brickyard. His mother felt it best not to overprotect him and she enjoyed his pride in a new pair of boots or in his first suspender trousers; she was pleased when he ''got along fine'' on his own.[3]

One of Jimmy's jobs was to look for the horses after they had been grazing for a day or two, a chore that required hours of walking. While they were waiting for the doctor to find a place for them, the children herded the horses, fetched milk and buttermilk from a nearby ranch, and played near the makeshift shelter. They were good children and Mat's will to endure was sustained by them.

Mat could count on only a few minor pleasures to

offset the uncertainties and fears of her existence. With snow falling three days before the end of May, she took the time to read a *Harper's* and looked forward to reading a Waverly novel that the doctor had brought from town. She could also take some satisfaction in knowing that they would be moving into Austin in a few days. The doctor had found a house to rent starting Saturday, June 16. He returned to the shelter by four o'clock, packed the wagon, and had the family in Austin by ten o'clock that evening. After unloading the wagon, the doctor, assisted by Mr. Pridham, went after another load, not returning until morning "completely tired out & the Dr half sick."[4]

The reason for the sudden haste in moving was an appointment the doctor had made for the following day to drive Colonel David Buel and a few others to Silver Bend and Hot Creek. This trip offered him the opportunity to prospect in the southeastern ranges while earning some money. Tired as he was from his Saturday's labors, the doctor went for Buel on Sunday morning, but had to return home when he learned that Buel was not ready to start. The postponement of the trip was just as well since the doctor's body was wracked with neuritic pains and, even with Mat's dutiful ministrations—blisters, mustards, chloroform, and quinine—he suffered intensely. A member of the Spires party, newly returned from Silver Bend, dropped in to relate glad tidings about a recently discovered ledge that was "the grandest thing in the world," but other than this, nothing else of value was reported.[5]

Dr. Gally was scheduled to leave Monday morning for the trip with Buel, but when he tried to drive the wagon, he found the pain was too great. He returned home and sent Mr. Pridham to Buel as his stand-in, a gesture that

Buel did not appreciate. Although Dr. Gally's knee was much improved by evening, it was too late to make the Silver Bend trip. As a less happy alternative, he decided to carry out his previous plan to cut hay.

The family would not move to Gilson's Park until July, and for the next three weeks, Mat and the children experienced some of the community life in Austin that they had been denied for many months, including visits with other women. Jimmy had helped the men decorate Bradford's Hall for a dance, but instead of attending, Mat listened to the music in bed. Except for the one walk into town with the doctor, she did not have his companionship. On June 21, Mat wrote:

> Last night the Dr. & I walked down below Cedar Street—it was my first view of the town & I was surprised at finding it so quiet. The Dr. was introduced to a Mr. Williams last night & discovered he was Anna Osborne's husband from Buffalo. He is here, agent for Iowa eastern company & talks of bringing Anna out. If he does so & we stay here, unless she has changed hugely or I have, I will [be] very glad.

Unless he was sick and needed attention, the doctor was rarely at home. Three or four times he spent all day in bed, once legitimately with neuritic pains. When he did not come home until early in the morning, and stayed in bed for the entire day, Mat noted tersely that he was very tired. With the hay work before him, he took an overnight fishing and hunting trip, conveying several friends in his wagon, and returned near midnight with fine trout, doves, and tasty lettuce.

During these weeks, the children fended for themselves. Jimmy sauntered around and liked to be where the action was, decorating for a dance or taking Matty to watch the dedication of the Methodist Church. The boy picked up a little money selling eggs and pot metal that he had melted down from old tin cans, but habitually he lost his earnings and other prized possessions. His mother fondly observed, when he reported the loss of a knife and pocketbook, that it was "an old business for him."[6] Matty was happy to run after anyone who would have her.

On the Fourth of July, a day with deep childhood memories for her father, Matty received an invitation to accompany him into town. The festivities were described by Mat:

> The procession consisted of Fenians, Firemen, Lander Guards, little children in a wagon to represent the States, 3 Ladies on horseback dressed respectively in Red White and Blue, mayor and city council, the orator of the day, citizens etc. Mr. B. P. Rankin made the oration. There was a horse race down in Clifton, target shooting on the road towards Emigrant Canon & a ball at the hall in the evening.

As usual, Mat missed out on the social event, but she had excitement enough when a fight took place in the house next door. A man brandishing a pistol invaded the home and threatened to kill its occupants, but he was prevented from carrying out his threats when several onlookers intervened.

By mid-July, the family was living at Gilson's ranch. The men—George Holland, Cal Joy, and Dr. Gally—expected to make several hundred dollars for several weeks' work, and there was sufficient incentive to settle down to the job. The doctor's spirit was sanguine, but his flesh was weak. Farming was work he had done in fits and starts and physically he was not hardened to the steady application that the work demanded. On the last day of

July, the men had ninety tons of hay cut and stacked, but the doctor's groin was sore, and he struggled to remain abreast of the other men.

At the end of the week, Dr. Gally headed for town to collect $600 in greenbacks from Edmonds & Ransom, which was a part payment for the hay crop. With cash in hand, he stood up at the bar with his Austin cronies. He did not arrive home until daylight, rather messed up as a result of "having tumbled from his horse into the creek and got wet and dirty enough." By the middle of August, he had been to the fields so irregularly that, after he was immobilized by "weakness in his bowels" and made quite uncomfortable by an "attack of colic or flatulency," he went into town to find someone to take his place with the sickle bar.[7]

During the last two weeks in August, the men worked steadily in the meadow. A terrific downpour on August 15 and more rain toward the end of the week worried everyone. Pools of water up to eight inches deep covered the grass, and some of the grass cut before the rain was completely submerged. The doctor employed more men to assist in stacking, and worked himself for short intervals. By noon on Monday, August 27, the job was finished.

From the moment they had left Austin for the hay ranch, Mat had less time to think about herself. Her mind was preoccupied with the work at the ranch, and at least once, she went out to the meadow to help the men. In addition, there were all kinds of little matters that needed her attention. Matty cut her leg on a sickle bar; Jimmy was seriously ill; and one of the horses bruised a leg attempting to break out of the stable.

Matters were not made easier by the hot work over

the ironing board in ninety-degree temperatures, the abominably oily water available for washing, a toothache that was agonizing until the doctor lanced her gum, the flies that plagued her in the house, and the grueling job of wrestling with the wash under a broiling sun. It had been a long time since she had anyone to help her with the chores. She had to scrub and clean the floor of the cabin and stand all day over a washtub or an ironing board. She tried to be patient, but she lost her temper in an argument with an emigrant woman. For someone who had known luxury and leisure, the change in her fortunes was indeed painful and would have been embarrassing were she among family and friends. For example, in nearly two years, Matty had worn but four pairs of shoes, and Mat had spent merely $38.75 on clothes for herself.[8]

The emigrants that came over the road in mid-July— some of them driving wagons in excellent shape—might have reminded her of the expectations with which she had started and which had long since turned to dust. The distant past of her childhood was remembered keenly when she received a letter from her father announcing that the childhood home had been sold to a Dr. Reeve for $10,000, an act which prompted her to write that "we've got no home any more."[9]

After the haying work was done, the sense of activity and the assurance that comes with employment vanished. The doctor was hardly ever around the place: elections were to be held in the autumn, and he was busy making political rounds. Mat had to stay up with him when he came home sick, as on the last day of August, when he returned and stated that he had eaten cabbage and onions and felt nauseous.

More and more during the first weeks of September,

Dr. Gally would be gone for two or three days without sending any word to Mat. When Mat did receive a message, it usually had an evasive tone. ''This afternoon,'' she recorded on September 8, ''lady & gentleman stopped in a buggy bringing us papers & provisions sent by the Dr did not know when he was coming home.''

In justice to Dr. Gally, it was common for the Victorian male not to consult with his wife about his business affairs. On the other hand, Mat, like many women of her generation, believed that men were inferior to women in their sense of loyalty and devotion. After an Austin woman committed suicide with an overdose of morphine, she declared that ''man's cruel unfaithfulness resulted as often before in a woman's ruin.''[10]

But Dr. Gally was fully occupied in seeking public office. Equipped with the summer's earnings and a realization of the infinite hardships of common frontier life, he wanted to pull himself up by his bootstraps. The primary election meetings of the Democrats and Republicans were being held in September, and he was actively promoting the goodwill of his many Austin friends. Mat might secretly have questioned the wisdom of many of her husband's moves, but her strong sense of loyalty prompted her to lend him encouragement while she put on a brave front.

The September days dragged on. News from home about Mat's father was not encouraging. Ailing, he had gone to the Upper Great Lakes to improve his health. She was happy for her sister Rebecca, who had given birth in August to a baby girl. The breaking up of the old ties with her family and past were felt in little ways. The loss of a thimble, for example, elicited poignant regret. She noted: ''I dropped my thimble down the well, can see, but cannot get it—it was my mother's thimble."[11]

As they waited for the doctor to make living arrangements for them in Austin again, the children spent their days studying, riding, and running errands, but Mat found that "the days are long and sometimes quite lonesome."[12] She was expecting the doctor to return on Thursday, September 20; she watched the road all day, hoping to catch sight of him before the sun set, but he did not appear. Already the nights were turning chilly, and Thursday night saw the water freeze in the tubs to a thickness of one-quarter inch. On the same night, she recalled that two years had come and gone since they had camped at the crest of Egan Canyon. Like that earlier time, they stood again at the divide between old disappointments and visions of a happier future.

The doctor arrived home on Friday. He announced that he had to relinquish the hay ranch immediately, a fact evidenced by the arrival of the new occupants early in the day. They moved their possessions out of the cabin and Mat sat outside while the wind blew disagreeably. Dr. Gally and Jimmy went to find the horses, but they succeeded in locating only one, a horse they called Jule.

Because the family could not leave that night, the doctor dragged the mattress into the warehouse where Mat and the children were to sleep. He drank some coffee and started out in the dark to track down the horses. Mat wondered when he would be back, observing that "he is so troubled and so busy & so anxious to be in town."[13] By eight o'clock the next morning, he had returned with the horses, and in short order had them in harness. He brought the family and some of their possessions on that cold Saturday, September 22, to the house he had bought in Austin.

The Gallys were inside the house by nine o'clock, but they had no opportunity to see what they had until the following day. The doctor had bought the property in upper Austin from Elias C. Brearley, a Lander County attorney, for the price of their horse, Tobe, whom Mat estimated to be worth from $250 to $300. Upon inspection of the house in broad daylight, Mat saw that it was small and the rooms were tiny, but the size of the lot allowed for adding a room. Soft water was available, which was a positive luxury. The narrow room where she prepared breakfast heated up quickly from the stove, however, and with the warmth of the late September morning sun, the morning meal was a stifling affair. The next few days were busy ones as the family settled into their new home.

The doctor's plans were taking shape, too, and a few days after the Gallys' return to Austin, the Democrats held their county convention and nominated Dr. Gally as their candidate for state senator. With this important matter disposed of favorably, the doctor made ready for a prospecting trip to the southeast with three other men. Late Friday morning, September 25, they left in the doctor's wagon, planning to be away for two weeks. The weather, "fit for Elysium," was ideal for a trip of this kind. It took the men four days to travel to the small mining camp of Hot Creek, which was about 110 miles southeast of Austin. This was the first of two trips to Hot Creek in the autumn of 1866 that had momentous consequences for the Gally family.

During the doctor's prospecting tour, Mat employed herself with domestic tasks. She took the doctor's castaway pants and cut them down into trousers for Jimmy; she made soap for their own needs, sewed, scrubbed the floors, and instructed Matty in making her first apron. A letter from Hatty, dated September 15 and arriving in Austin on Monday, October 8, caused her some anxiety. Rebecca's baby, Alice, was reported sick "and they fear the result." Her father had not benefited from the trip to the Great Lakes and his health remained poor. Her brother George, by now a member of Boston's Brahmin circle, was traveling with Lilla in Switzerland. Three days before the arrival of the letter, Mat rememberd that "six years ago today my little King was born." On the Monday on which the letter from Hatty arrived, she had the doldrums. "I was sick until night," she confided to her diary on October 8, "though I sewed as well as I could. The days seem long and lonesome."

* * *

A time of renewed expectation was not far away, however. The night before the doctor returned from Hot Creek, flushed with the discoveries and claims he had made in the new Eldorado of Hot Creek, the people of Austin welcomed in the political season. Mat could hear the resounding vibration of cannon fire and had a glimpse of a rousing torchlight procession that featured voices and banners raised to Dixie. The speechifying was accompanied by a veritable din from the volume of huzzas, "the mills whistling & the boys screaming."[14]

A year before, the doctor had run on the Democratic ticket for a seat in the state assembly, but he had lost with the other incumbents on his party's ticket. The Democrats could not overcome in that election the stigma of being the party of rebellion. In the election of 1866, the Democrats in Lander County wrestled again with the charge that the party was tainted with treason.

The Fourteenth Amendment, passed by Congress on June 13, 1866, and ratified by the states on July 28, 1868, reinforced the charge and constituted the rallying point for the state campaign. During the Lander County campaign, the Democratic party strenuously opposed section 3 of the amendment, which disbarred from office former federal and state officeholders who had aided the Confederacy. Southern sympathizers in Nevada pointed out that it would make all of the prominent and leading Democrats in the South ineligible to hold public office and thus would restrict Southern political power. The Republicans, avowing allegiance to the congressional plan of reconstruction, affirmed that the disbarment of the rebel leaders from their former political power was a temporary disability to be removed at the discretion of Congress.[15]

The Democrats also opposed, but less vigorously, section 2 of the amendment reducing congressional representation unless the Southern states permitted Negro suffrage.[16] The *Reese River Reveille* editorialized on September 22 that before the Civil War, a Negro had been counted for purposes of representation as three-fifths of a white person, "without any political rights, giving their masters an unfair proportion of power in the government." The Democrats and the South claimed that now that the war was over, all Negroes, or the other two-fifths, should be counted for purposes of representation, yet should not be entitled to the ballot.[17] The Republicans resented the unfair advantage the South would gain in Congress from chattel representation, and the proposal was described by a *Reveille* correspondent on August 13 as "unreasonable not to say insolent and impudent."

The first section of the amendment, conferring state and federal citizenship upon all persons born or naturalized in the United States, was far more controversial than the second or third sections. Nevertheless, Republican support of section 1 of the amendment, spurred by a spirit of loyalty to the party and its plan of reconstruction, appeared in the columns of the *Reveille* during the peak of the campaign. [18]

Of paramount importance to the outcome of the election was the Democratic contention that the amendment was unconstitutional on the grounds that the absence of Southern states in the Congress invalidated the action pertaining to them. At a Democratic meeting in October, Henry K. Mitchell, a candidate for office, charged that Congress had violated the Constitution by "depriving States, without their consent, of equal suffrage in the Senate." [19] On August 21, the *Reveille* published the official pro-Southern position of the Johnson "Bread and Butter" party, which the Democrats used in the campaign to advance their case. The position stated that the states can by no act of rebellion forfeit their right to representation in Congress since "representation is, under the Constitution not only expressly recognized as a right but is imposed as a duty, and it is essential in both aspects to the existence of the Government, and maintenance of its authority."

The Republicans, who saw ratification of the amendment by the states still out of the Union as a condition for readmission, vehemently disputed the claim that the amendment was unconstitutional. Their reasoning was that as long as a state retained its constitutional relationship with the government of the United States, it could not be deprived of representation in Congress. But if, by its own actions, a state destroyed that relationship, it then deprived itself of its former rights. [20]

The Union Party of Lander County jubilantly supported the shibboleths of the new political and social equality. It was distinctly jingoistic in crying for measures "to rebuke the selfish and calculating tyranny of England, and to defeat the grasping ambition of France."[21] More pertinent for Nevada politics was the pledge to keep the home fires burning by excluding the old Democrats from the seat of power.

Dr. Gally was running against D. W. Welty for the long-term state senate seat, and he spent most of his time downtown, entertaining himself with whisky and politics. He had work to do around the house, building a fence and adding a room to the dwelling, but he drifted away from these jobs. Mr. Bell and Jimmy did most of the work on the new room, and the doctor steeled himself for what he hoped would be his imminent victory at the polls. Mat, knowing the course of events from previous experience, busied herself as much as she could. "Somehow I worked hard all day—the wind blows chill," reads the entry in her diary for Sunday, October 14.

On Wednesday evening at about seven o'clock, Dr. Gally came home inebriated and fell into bed. Even the appeal of a friend to make a speech at a meeting that night could not rouse him. "Alas the frailty of human kind," observed Mat. The nature of the problem would unfold with time. The meeting took place as scheduled, without the doctor, who was reported incapacitated by a severe cold. The Austin band provided the music, and Henry K. Mitchell, a Democratic nominee for Congress, provided the oratory. Mitchell impugned Governor Nye for saying that within a year the Negro would possess the suffrage with white men in Nevada. Someone in the crowd exclaimed, "'Bully for Nye,'" to which the speaker retorted: "'Yes, it would be bully. And if the principles of Nye and Ashley obtained, it would not only be bully, it would be wooly.'"[22]

The following day, the doctor remained in bed until evening when the whole family went to town in the wagon to listen to the speeches. Mitchell was matched against Fitch, the Union party nominee for Congress in 1864. With every argument made by Fitch, the Union men fired off a cannon that was mounted on a hill, while the Democratic men applauded their man by hammering on anvils. After the rousing meeting of the previous evening, the doctor pleaded sickness on Friday morning, left the work at the house to Mr. Bell, and went downtown to celebrate the forthcoming victory at the polls with his cronies. He returned home drunk about six o'clock in the evening. "I wonder," wrote Mat in her diary on the same evening, "what will be the end of my miserable life—only for my little children have I any hope or courage."[23]

After this last disastrous episode, the doctor settled down to working on the house during the days and to politicking at night. As Election Day, November 6, neared, the tempo of the electioneering picked up. On Monday evening, October 29, John Garber and Dr. Gally spoke at a Democratic rally. By this time, the doctor was fairly well known for his jocularity. On this particular evening, he was holding out against the Fourteenth Amendment, pronouncing "the business of amending the Constitution bad and uncalled for," but his audience was delighted not so much by the content of his remarks, as by the ease of his wit. The *Reveille* reported that "at the conclusion of his speech, the amiable doctor—who belongs to the school of laughing philosophers—sat down amid cheers and laughter."[24]

Not even a bad cold could keep Dr. Gally away from politics for more than one night. He caught a cold while working on the roof all day Monday, and as usual when he was not feeling well, he wanted Mat to nurse him. She obliged: "I had him gargle quantities paregoric & ginger, put a big mustard plaster on him & after a while he went to sleep."[25] He was much improved in the morning and pushed his campaign into the outlying mining districts, making a speech at Yankee Blade that evening.

While the doctor went to Yankee Blade, Mat went over to stay with Mrs. Billy Brown, a sick neighbor woman whom she had promised to help out. When she arrived, she was surprised to see the "elegant Mrs. Charley Spires & was politely informed that I was not wanted so I ran up home alone in the dark." The rebuff hurt more than a little, since she had left Jimmy sick at home to do an act of kindness for a neighbor.

The doctor continued his campaign in the Reese River Mining District almost up to election eve. The reports coming in indicated that he had a good chance of being elected, and there had been a large crowd to listen to him at Big Creek. By Saturday, November 3, he was home, and the family went down in the wagon to the Democratic rally. A stand had been built to accommodate the ladies, who were treated to a spectacular event. "Little pyramids of nut pine," observed the local columnist, "crackled and blazed; anvils imitated theatrical thunder; rockets hissed and fizzled and exploded in colors of crimson, gold, and green, and occasionally terminated in a wriggling serpent."[26] The wind, which had been blowing earlier in the evening, increased in ferocity and drove the smoke from the bonfires into the ranks of the spectators, practically blinding everyone. The speakers were Rhodes, the Democratic candidate for state attorney general, and Frank Hereford, the doctor's running mate for state senator, whom Mat thought made the best speech she had heard that year.[27] By nine o'clock the Gallys were home, but were unable to sleep while anxiously wondering whether the blowing wind would rip off the roof.

In the two days that remained until the election, the doctor fussed around in town. He was late in coming home on Sunday, November 4, even though it was Matty's eighth birthday. The following day, he was downtown again, leaving Bell to work on the house, but he did manage to forget politics long enough to buy the groceries for the winter months. Election day was Tuesday, November 6, and, at least among friends, the prediction was that Gally would be elected state senator.

The returns were in by the following day: the Republicans made a clean sweep of the major political offices,[28] and Dr. Gally lost to D. W. Welty. The doctor had left the house early election evening and did not come home that night or the following day. His friend Bell searched for him, but without success. With no news of his whereabouts by seven o'clock that evening, Mat wrote on November 7 in her diary: "Drunk I suppose, asleep in the livery stable I know. Mr. Bell has put in the day running after him." Not until Thursday morning did Bell succeed with considerable trouble in bringing his inebriated friend home, where he slept for several hours.

The nature of the problem stemming from the Lander County convention was disclosed by the doctor in an article written in 1870. He read in the Elko *Independent* of allegations made against him by a Democrat who charged that he was bidding for Republican office. Dr. Gally wrote in response:

> The truth is, I was never in nor near any political convention in this State, either after office or otherwise, except in the Lander County Democratic Convention of 1866; and at that time I wanted to be Recorder of Lander County because I had done a good deal of rough work for the party; but the Democratic-loving Democracy gave the office to the then ''Black Republican'' County Clerk, because, as they said, he had made a big winning at William Gorman's faro bank, and would be an influential ''flop.''
>
> How's that for high in a white working man's Democratic party? Not very terrible, of course, but then it's all true. . . .
>
> The Democracy of Lander thrust the nomination of State Senator upon me in 1866, to help cover up the nomination of the black Republican Clerk as Democratic Recorder and hold the party together.[29]

With this defiant bust, Dr. Gally rang out two years of frontiering in sagebrush land.

cA Fresh
Venture

D R. GALLY quickly dismissed from his mind his political defeat, and within a few days he was making plans to follow up on the discoveries made during October in the Danville and Hot Creek districts to the southeast of Austin. Mat was within a few days of being thirty-two years old and he was nearly forty, but neither his age nor his reverses dampened his enthusiasm. He had fallen completely into the dilemma of the independent poor man of Nevada. Without the money to get started in a profitable enterprise, he looked for silver ledges and hoped to sell one of them to someone with money.

The most enticing feature of this way of life was the freedom it offered to be one's own man. All the troubles and hardships the Gallys had endured as a family were reduced to near insignificance as he looked optimistically to the future. ''Of course we have our own troubles like other people,'' he wrote to his father-in-law, ''but we early trained ourselves to handle our own troubles from birth to death—so we get along."[1]

As he packed his gear to leave on Sunday, November 11, 1866, Dr. Gally certainly was aware of the distress the prospect of an absence of three or four weeks would create. The night before his departure, Jimmy was sick and Mat was showing the strain his absences always created. Nevertheless, on Monday he left Austin for Danville. The day after his departure, the weather turned cold, and Mat thought of him on the road as she wrote in her diary: "The gentry have a bad beginning for their journey—camping out such weather no joke."[2] Fortunately, the following day was clear and pleasant.

The doctor was making the second trip to the southeast with prospector friends Adams, Dennis, Bell, Rockyfellow, and Mills. The party proceeded up Main Street, through Austin, and struggled up the rocky summit of the Toiyabe, which was covered with snow. Scattered birch, willow, and cottonwood trees broke the monotony of snow and sky. The eastern slope of the range led into Smoky Valley, which derived its name from the haze that hangs over the valley floor. From any point in the valley, the Toiyabe could be seen framing the horizon and, in the eye of the travelers, blocked out the world of men. Salt and alkali, "the brown, dry valley, and the tall, snowy mountains" imparted a "sense of loneliness and weak humanity."[3]

But a prospecting party of six men in Nevada, with the weather anywhere near passable, was a jolly affair, especially if one of the members of the party was a wag. Such a character was the unnamed "doctor," whom David E. Buel and Mahlon D. Fairchild had met in Smoky Valley. Their traveling companion kept everyone in good humor "by the peculiar manner in which he 'persuaded' his jaded mustangs to keep pace with ours. And he did it, but 'by the gods,' he 'warmed 'em' with 'four dollar whips' and willow 'twigs,' until a stranger would have sworn while looking at his load, that he was some itinerant vender of splint brooms.''[4]

After a day of riding over the valley floor or working one's way into the foothills leading up into the canyons, appetites were keen and bodies were tired. When a halt was called, one of the party gathered ''rabbit-brush''; someone else built a fire and put on the coffeepot, made bread, and sliced down the slab of bacon; and the others went to look after the stock. With sufficient wood chopped to keep the fire burning late into the night, the men settled down to the meal. ''That supper, in a city or a well-regulated family anywhere,'' recalled the doctor, ''would have been a failure; but exercise and the open air make a compound sauce which renders 'sad' bread, stale bacon, and black coffee, a very desirable feast.'' As was the habit of prospectors, when the meal was done, the pipes came out and the conversation ranged from the most improbable yarns to snake stories and Kanaka girls. Sometimes, the night was whiled away ''with wine, and mirth, and song.''[5]

From Smoky Valley, the travelers headed for the Toquima Range, which leads into Monitor Valley to the east. By Thursday they were within twenty miles of Danville. They had not covered much ground in five days of traveling and probably were slowed by the struggle to move the wagon over the muddy summits. By the end of the week, the Gally party had ascended the Monitor Range and had come down the eastern slope to the Danville district.[6]

In Danville, the doctor found a ledge to his liking

which measured fifteen feet wide and was "the largest I ever saw."[7] Before returning to Austin, he dug enough rock to bring back some for an assay. After spending two weeks in the Danville district, the men covered the twenty miles to the Hot Creek mines, where some members of the party had located ledges earlier in the autumn.[8]

The Hot Creek district had been organized in February, 1866, and by September, a hundred men were residing there. A number of promising mines were being opened: the Indian Jim mine, located the previous April, for example, was reported to have "50,000 tons of milling ore estimated to be in sight."[9] The canyon wall exposed a cross section of the vein, which measured 600 feet long and 60 feet wide. "Nature," declared the *Reveille*, "seems in this instance to have given the miner an example of her method of opening a vein on a grand scale."[10]

The Indian Jim, which was the pride of Hot Creek, had sold for $50,000 to capitalists, with the original locators holding a one-fifth interest in it. To work the ore, a mill had been erected in November by the Consolidated Silver Mining Company. Scattered throughout the district were other locations with exciting possibilities: the Old Dominion, rich in horn silver, assayed from $100 to $5,000 per ton; the Silver Glance was abundant in black sulphuret and native silver; the American Hunter was running assays varying from $40 to $1,000 per ton; and both the Shenandoah and Gazelle were showing promise.[11]

To question the potential wealth of the Hot Creek district bordered on heresy. A mining expert, Professor Peter Duckfoot, had visited Hot Creek and had come away doubting the value of the mines there. The preposterous Duckfoot or Duckworth, "Professor of

Humbug and Grand Quackery in the State of Nevada, and
self-appointed Mining Prophet and Deep Shaft Astrologer
in the counties of Lander and Nye in said State,'' based
his opinion on a clairvoyant session with ''the spirit of his
departed grandmother,'' who knew ''the ledges will *peter*,
because, as she says, everything has an end.'' [12]

Even the most optimistic individual in the district
could not tell the extent of the chloride ore in the mines
already located. It was evident that the surface chloride
ore was rich, but there was no way of ascertaining the
depth of the ore deposits. Those who believed in the
district contended that the abundant limestone was a cap
that covered formations of talcose slate, granite, gneiss,
and porphyry. But the state mineralogist, in his 1866
Report, observed that the situation at Hot Creek was a
mixed one: some of the lodes, where the limestone had
been weathered, looked impressive, but where the ledge
could be seen through a crop out, ''the mineral appears in
small seams, as if struggling to reach the surface.'' [13]

The crux of the problem was the depth and breadth of
the mineral belts in this part of Nevada. The earliest
reports of the ledges at Northumberland, Danville, Hot
Creek, and Reveille created, according to the state
mineralogist, a sense of ''incredibility.'' Miners in the
Reveille district were talking of veins of ''immense
proportions,'' thicknesses varying from forty feet in the
Atlantic Mine to 106 feet in the Crescent. Knowledgeable
mining men were skeptical, pointing out that mineral was
being found in limestone and that a regular vein system
had not been disclosed.

The next few years would reveal the narrow base of
the discoveries: most of the silver ore came from the
surface limestone rather than from more substantial ore

deposits. The hopeful discoverers had before them a few years of success at best. Where one company was able to gain control of a major part of a district, as at Morey, the working of the irregularly distributed surface ore was profitable. Prospectors and independent miners were enormously impressed by surface appearances, and in 1866, 1867, and 1868, the hopes of these men were inflated, and they tramped through the country exulting in the good times ahead.[14]

In October, the doctor staked claims on three ledges, and the assays run on the ore showed a favorable return on two of them. He was elated by the possibilities the future held, but much work had to be done in interesting men with money in the ledges. The outside mining districts like Danville, Morey, Hot Creek, Empire, and Reveille were staked out by impecunious men. Preliminary excavation work and prospecting could be done while awaiting developments. The same poverty of means existed in the Philadelphia district or the Silver Bend mines, thirty-five miles west of Hot Creek on the western slope of the Toquima Range. The ore of the Highbridge mine in this area assayed from $200 to $3,000 per ton and was bought from Colonel D. E. Buel by the Combination Silver Mining Company of New York for a few thousand dollars.[15]

Dr. Gally recognized that there was a good deal of risk involved in the venture, and he summed up the alternatives in one sentence: "If I make money here I will make a good deal of money, but if I do not make a good deal I will not make any out of the mines." Past misjudgments were buried in his memory when he added: "These are the first mines out of thousands I have seen that I have spent much time or any amt of money on."[16]

As the doctor became more familiar with Hot Creek on this second trip, he could not fail to see the positive natural attractions of the place. It was different from any of the other settlements he had known in the past two years. More than a hundred miles southeast of Austin, Hot Creek is much warmer than is Austin. The canyon itself presents a striking contrast to the dry, sombre sagebrush that surrounds it, and plants grow there that are not commonly found in Nevada: grasses, sunflowers, and willows cover the ground; and reeds, tule, and cattail flags flourish in marshes fed by springs. The profusion of plant life is watered both by a stream which originates in a hot spring located on the western slope of the Hot Creek Range and by the cold springs in the area.[17]

The speed with which prospectors had explored the central basin region from the Humboldt River in the north to the Colorado River in the south opened a vast region for settlement. No one took time to be cautious, to ask questions, or to await developments. No sooner had the prospectors announced their discoveries than parties of miners followed in their wake. A year before, the prospectors had to feel their way from one watering spot to another; but in November, 1866, the canyons and the natural passes as well as the stopping places for forage and water were known.

To facilitate the movement of men, supplies, and silver ore, enterprising men were laying out toll roads. Stonebarger, for example, was laying out a toll road between Austin and Hot Creek in September, utilizing a natural road that passed through the canyons connecting the Smoky, Monitor, Fish Spring, and Hot Creek valleys. By the end of December, Stonebarger still had considerable work ahead of him in grading the summit of

Clipper Gap, which connected Smoky and Monitor valleys, and he had to do something about the marshes in Hot Creek Canyon to make this pass serviceable for heavy wagons. Before the Stonebarger Road was completed, however, a competitor by the name of Rutherford had entered the field.[18]

These indications of active enterprise strengthened Dr. Gally's belief in the future of the southeastern mines; dreaming of success, he prepared to return to Austin. It was an exhilarating return trip and even the weather, with the exception of a few days, was delightful. As Dr. Gally recalled, with a flamboyant rhetorical flourish a few years later, "we wandered, like forlorn and foolhardy knights-errant, to the cheerful music of industrious Spanish spurs, on long, bony steeds, zigzagging through the pathless artemesia, while summer heat or winter snow made night and pancakes welcome as a banquet of the rich, and dusty blankets 'silvered i' the moon,' couches of down in Dreamlands castle halls."[19]

The first real winter storms in the Reese River country broke while the doctor was on the road. Three nights before he arrived home, a fierce blizzard drove across the country. Mat stayed up listening to the furious lashing of the wind. "It blew the snow," she recorded, "through every crevice & cranny—the canvas roof leaked sadly. I was obliged to cut a hole in the back room ceiling so that I could put in my hand & draw out great balls of snow—it was quite noon before I got the house moderately dry."[20]

For Mat, the weeks of the doctor's absence had been long and weary ones. Outside the daily routine of housework, there was not much she could look forward to with any certainty. She sewed, working on a flannel undershirt for the doctor and pantaloons for Jimmy; baked bread, cake, and pies with the children's help; stitched a petticoat and frock for Matty; helped out with one of the neighbor's sick children; and covered a mattress.

No matter how busy Mat was, the hours and days passed slowly. She visited and received visits from the neighbor women, which helped her forget her loneliness for a few hours. The solitude made her think of the old times. One November evening after an Indian summer day, a full moon and a warm night had her writing that "this day so soft & fair makes me lonesome & homesick."[21] The whole burden of her isolation came down on her heavily at the beginning of December after the doctor had been away three weeks. It was Sunday, December 2, and Mat noted: "We have read talked played and yet the day is dull long and tedious." In a wave of self-pity, she revealed the depth of her emotion. "We are lonesome," she entered in the diary, "there is no one coming in and out. Women & children get tired alone."

As Mat endured poverty and hardships, she began to feel a terrifying sense that her sacrifices were in vain. She recalled the doctor's ruinous trip to the headwaters of the Humboldt River two years before, and the months of hardship at Roberts Creek during the past winter were still fresh in her mind. She realized that the family's situation was not likely to improve. Mat was simply trapped by frontier life; what she wanted was the security of settled middle-class life.

On Wednesday, December 5, the doctor still had not returned. She had heard from a passer-by that a week before he had gone to Hot Creek, but she had received no word about when he would start for Austin. Mat concluded that "at this rate there is no telling when they'll be here." As Mat and the children were eating supper Thursday evening, they were interrupted by someone at the door. It was Bell, who was followed by Adams, Dennis, and Dr. Gally. They had arrived on the doctor's birthday in good health, and they were happy and optimistic. They radiated cheer and good humor, talking about the excellent ledges they had and the opening value they were showing. The doctor wanted to return to Hot Creek within a few weeks, and Mat's unwillingness to remain in Austin without him made the family's move to Hot Creek certain.

Mat rushed around trying to tackle fifty jobs at once, and the doctor completed the necessary business prior to moving the family. The two wagons were packed by the middle of the week, and on Thursday afternoon, December 13, the Gallys and Bell rumbled out of Austin headed for the mines to the southeast.

At the Summit House on their way over the mountains, the travelers encountered Tom, who was on his way to Austin from the Roberts Creek ranch. That night, they camped in several inches of snow. Snow was falling the next day as they pulled across Smoky Valley towards Clipper Gap, the pass in the Toquima Range that led into Monitor Valley. The snow had stopped falling when they reached the eastern portion of the valley, but the horses had a difficult time pulling the wagons through the sand. Mat's wagon and team, not as heavily loaded as the doctor's, moved in advance, heading for a wood chopper's cabin at the entrance to the Gap. They did not reach the cabin before night, however, and spent the night in the cold. In her diary for December 14, Mat wrote:

> By this time it was dark & bitter cold, & about 20 rods
> from the cabin, Punch took one of her tantrums & would

not pull for us. We unhitched the horses, let the wagon
stand. Mr. Bell after some trouble started a fire & then
went back to the Dr with the horses—things looked
mighty dismal, but the children & I piled on wood of
which there was fortunately an abundance, & by the time
the Dr arrived had a bright fire & were thoroughly
thawed ourselves. He soon made the horses bring up the
other wagon & we laid down the beds, got supper which
we ate with a gusto, turned out the horses & went to
sleep. We watered at the well belonging to the house into
which the McCrackens moved, they were not very
gracious.

The snow was falling again when they awoke on
Saturday morning. After breakfast, the doctor teamed up
all the horses and pulled one of the wagons over the pass,
returning in about an hour for the other wagon. By
evening, they were in Monitor Valley, which seemed
much warmer than Smoky Valley, and even spending the
night out of doors was not unpleasant. Mat observed with
some pride that she ''was the first white woman who had
ever seen that valley which is called Monitor.''

The Gallys hoped to reach the Monitor Range on
Sunday, December 16, but it was to be a difficult march.
Mat described the journey:

The road was heavy, we were obliged to ''double teams''
once or twice. The snow 6 or 7 inches deep, so we made
a dry camp after dark at about 8 o'clk. The moon was
full & bright but the cold was severe. We jumped out.
The Dr shoveled & I swept the snow away to make a dry
place for the fire & tent, but the shavings wouldn't burn
so we pulled out the oil can & saturated the wood with
kerosene & lo! a blaze. We soon had a famous fire plenty
of wood lying all around us. Matty had walked got her
feet wet & was crying with the cold. I had her bare &
rub[bed] them & put them in a big muff. James stood it
like a man.

Monday they crossed the Monitor Range or the Danville Mountain. They drove until late at night, halting when they came to a deserted cabin ''with an excuse for a chimney but were so cold that it seemed grand to us.'' After tending to the horses, they had supper and went to sleep, happy they had some shelter—poor though it was.

The travelers spent the better part of Tuesday hunting the horses. All in all they had a miserable time:

> Presently I found all the horses were in sight but Beck. About 2 P.M. they came back almost stiff & tired out, but no Beck. They could see where she had rolled near the edge of precipice & concluded she had tumbled off. We all gave her up for dead, but the Dr said she must be found dead or alive. So Mr. B set off again & in about an hour while the Dr was across the canon cutting wood for the night who should appear but Mr. B and Beck. She seemed pretty well so we got supper hitched up & started for Danville creek 5 miles off. After a long tedious cold drive directly in the teeth of a sharp wind we made Danville about 9 o'clk P.M. Here there is a station etc. The Dr had the horses stabled put up the tent & I crawled into bed feeling wretchedly. The children were wrapped in blankets in the wagon & lifted them into bed. They both woke up & ate some supper with the gents, but I was half sick with cold. The snow on the mountain was over a foot deep but at Danville only an inch or two. You may believe we were rejoiced to see Beck alive & well.

In six days they had covered seventy miles, and they had still to cross Fish Spring Valley and the Hot Creek Range. Again, Mat's diary tells the story:

> Wednesday. Got off pretty well in the morning which was clear but a cold wind in our faces. We had now about 30 miles to our journey's end. The road was heavy the snow being ground into the heavy sand. We started in the wagons leaving Mr. Bell to come on with the pony.

Presently Matty discovered she had lost her muff, which we valued because it had been used by Mother. The Dr went back a mile or two & not seeing it concluded an Indian had captured it. By & by along came Mr. B on the pony, muff on his arm. We drove until nearly dark & made a dry camp 10 or 12 miles from Hot Creek. The horses had excellent grass & ate close to camp.

On Thursday, December 20, the journey was almost over. A wet snow fell as they entered Hot Creek Canyon, and the horses had a hard pull. The road was treacherously soft, and the wagon Dr. Gally was driving unavoidably hit a place where the wheels settled to their hubs. By doubling teams and with much effort, he succeeded in freeing the wagon. It was nearly mid-afternoon before they came to the cabin they were to occupy in the lower canyon, but they had to leave the wagons and cross the creek to get to it. The cabin walls were made of sod and the roof of dirt; a spring, providing soft water for washing, was nearby. After the rough camping of the past eight days, Mat declared that the dwelling "seemed fine to us." The bad weather had blown over and the day of their arrival was warm and pleasant.

In a letter to his father-in-law, the doctor discussed his hopes for his new venture. He was banking heavily on his belief that the Hot Creek district would open up. With claims to three ledges (with one of the ledges near a millsite), two town lots, and 160 acres of woodland, the doctor had not overlooked future possibilities. Rather nostalgically, he recalled that he had an opportunity to invest in the "celebrated Murphy Mine at Twin River which is now grinding out three thousand dollar[s] per day of clear coin, and is quoted in New York at $122½ per foot." In a mellow, philosophizing mood, he wrote

George James that he wished he would live "untill we can all receive your congratulations upon our prosperity; but if we do not arrive at that blissful period you may rest assured that no family has better learned the lesson of life than we."[22]

Mat did not complain about the trip to Hot Creek, for it had been her choice to accompany her husband. The burdens of isolation, poverty, and suffering had made of her a supreme realist. Had she remained in Austin, she would have escaped the rigors of pioneering and might have restrained her husband from another plunge into the quicksands of the prospector's optimism. But the fear of loneliness and the heartache of separation decided her fate. The Hot Creek trip was the beginning of a new adventure which would hold many tribulations for Mat Gally.

7

The Hot Creek Settlement

THEIR FIRST Christmas at Hot Creek, in 1866, was as "warm as springtime." It was a much happier Christmas than the one they were hardly aware of the previous year at Roberts Creek. The doctor invited two of his friends, Rockyfellow and Cooke, to a festive dinner that Mat had ready by four o'clock. She served "roast mutton, cabbage, potatoes, turnips & carrots, pickles, jelly, cold bread & hot biscuit, tea & coffee, with an apple pudding." Mat was quite proud of her accomplishment, "not a home dinner by any means, but tolerable for so new a town. I was tired when night came. Oh ho for my father's house."[1]

There was much work to be done in getting settled. The Gallys had to build a house of their own, and the first weeks at Hot Creek were spent in cutting timber. The doctor had considerable help from Bell and Rockyfellow in putting up the structure; but he took much pleasure in the work, from laying out the lot to making the door frames and putting in the ridge pole and the rafters. The most time-consuming part of the job was obtaining the logs, and on many a night the men straggled in long after dark, having spent the day cutting timber. By the beginning of February their roughhewn log cabin was completed and they moved in. It stood on a flat outside the canyon; above it was the middle village, and at the summit of the range was the upper settlement.

The hum of activity at Hot Creek encouraged the Gallys and spurred them to new activity. The Indian Jim mine was producing ore and sustaining the reputation of the district. The doctor was elated by the interest his properties were attracting. The surface ore from the mine he had opened at Danville was assaying at $48 per ton, and capitalists from the East who had examined it were talking of putting up a mill in the spring to work the ore. A small mill, the Old Dominion, was completed and operating shortly after the Gallys arrived at Hot Creek. The pounding of the stamps had a pleasing sound. "To a stranger's ear," wrote the doctor, "this ceaseless rhythmic roar in the otherwise silent land becomes at first a sort of grand, loud, yet muffled harmony; then a painful, thundering discord; still later a bearable monotony; and, finally, the agreeable pulsating music of prosperity."[2]

To the experienced eye of Dr. Gally, the camp was thriving. Up and down the canyon were the log, stone, and canvas shelters of the bachelor miners who made the hills resound with their boisterous shouts. The road through the canyon was Main Street, a meeting place for men coming in and going out. In a small community such as Hot Creek, which boasted a store, two saloons, and a blacksmith's shop, inhabitants were well acquainted with one another. Men congregated in the middle village, known as Carrollton, for socializing, some of them in the streets and others in the local store or the saloons "reading (for miners read the news and support newspapers)—playing cards—annecdotizing or philosophizing."[3] The friendly atmosphere of the store and saloon, heightened by the warmth of a glowing stove on cold days, stimulated conversation. Dr. Gally wrote a lively description of the saloon:

> On such a day the saloon, by which we mean the whisky-mill, is the head-quarters—perhaps, more exactly, the stomach-quarters—of mountain society. Here is comfort—the truth is the truth! Here is warmth, and seats, good cheer, bad language, old jokes, new jokes, all sorts of character, and a thoroughly entrenched scorn of the howling, white-robed battling of the elements. The hot water steams upon the stove; the alcoholic amusements shine behind their painted labels, like the well-groomed steeds of the sun-driver; the pale yellow of exotic limes and lemons rises in miniature pyramids on bases of upturned, crystal glasses at each side or in front of the great mirror, which reflects the supple shoulders, wriggling elbows, and elaborately done back-hair of the Adonis who mixes "the poisons" and polishes, with rapid napkin, the glittering goblet, whose late contents cost the buyer just "two bits," or a quarter of a dollar. Here are newspapers of all sorts, from all parts, in several languages; a place to sit yourself down and put your North American feet as high as your centennial head, while the backs of your legs, away up, are comforted by the glowing stove as you absorb the news of many lands. Here are pictures on the walls, some of which are valuable as art, and others which show to the artistic mind that art is valuable—when you find it.
>   Here the isolate wits of the camp come with their newest "good thing"; and here the anxious,

unappreciative man comes, day after day, in his hopeless
hunt after what it is that "the fellers laugh so damnation
loud at," when he "don't see nothin'." Here is the
charming fellow who is not only unconsciously "witty in
himself, but the cause of that which wit is in other men."
Here is the club, the lecture room, the town meeting, the
academy, and the forum of the camp.[4]

The typical prospector of a small outside camp such
as Hot Creek, as Dr. Gally saw him, was somewhat rough
but was not a "gawk or booby" and was always willing
to learn. These men could, when the mood was upon
them, "drink and fight like the souls in Walhalla,"[5] and
even on weekdays, drunken, noisy men could be found
out on the street. On holidays, high spirits could be
expected to lead to fights. On July 4, 1867, Martha
recorded in her diary that a "Mr. Bond jumped on Mr.
Twain, then on Rocky, and afterwards on Mr. Tipton,
whom he nearly killed."

Except for occasional drunkenness, Hot Creek was a
quiet place.[6] A rare disturbance occurred four months
after the Gallys arrived in Hot Creek, and Mat called it
"quite an 'episode.'" The doctor had left early in
the morning, and Mat, after giving the children a midday
dinner, lay down in the back room. An intruder, who
appeared to be drunk, entered the front room and
summoned her in a "strange manner"; she sprang from
the bed to face the man who was standing in the doorway
demanding a meal and a bed for the night, a request which
she promptly denied. Rebuffed, he unburdened himself of
his blankets and "pointed very wickedly at me what I
supposed to be a knife." Mat sent the children for their
neighbor, Mr. Twain, who forced him out after a struggle.
The stranger returned several times, and Mr. Twain and

Mr. Gerow gave him a thrashing and locked him up in a room for the night. The men sent him on his way the next morning, warning him not to return under any circumstances, since he already had made a general nuisance of himself by taking articles from several cabins.[7]

Mat was the recipient of much courtesy and deference in a place where she was—for a number of months—the only white woman. Mahlon D. Fairchild, who had been on a prospecting expedition to the southeast in December, 1866, saw Mat at Hot Creek and declared that she "can justly claim the honor of being the first white lady to venture southeast of Stonebarger's."[8] Many of the people who came through Hot Creek made a point of keeping Mat informed about the outside world. Prospectors and travelers stopped at the cabin to talk to her, and men in the camp told her about their troubles and discussed with her their plans for the future. The doctor undoubtedly was thinking of her when he had a character in one of his stories say:

> She was naturally motherly-like, and cheerful with everybody that came anigh her. She put the boys in mind of their mothers and elder sisters. Often we had the children with us, and some of them "boys" had left little ones of their own away back behind them, and they used to take to our children like fathers, until I got afraid they'd spoil them with presents, and odd talk to the boy about being a man and chewing tobacco and the like, and to the girl about which of them the child liked the most, and pertending that they'd fight about her, and all such carryings-on, for fun.[9]

A most welcome visitor in Hot Creek was Dr. Riddle. His base of operation was Belmont, but he traveled many miles in all directions to help the sick. He was a skillful medical practitioner and was a man without pretensions of any kind. Belmonters knew him as a wag and permitted him certain liberties in this role. Work for this mining doctor was challenging. Miners who fractured and broke limbs in bad falls in shafts were easy cases compared to the victims of knife fights or gangrene. Dr. Riddle was a superb surgeon who could amputate limbs, excise a tumor embedded in a lung, and clean out the track of a bullet wound.

A blasting accident that occurred at Morey, fifteen miles north of Hot Creek, brought Dr. Riddle over from Belmont. The report of serious injuries to a man's hands suggested the possibility of amputation. On the way to Morey, Dr. Riddle, accompanied by Dr. Murphy, stopped at the Gally cabin to talk and to borrow a sponge. The next day, May 11, the two men returned the sponge and told Mat that the man was in "reasonable condition though losing all the fingers of the right hand & one of the left hand." A few days after the operation, a messenger was sent from Morey to obtain morphine and laudanum for the sick man. Weeks later, Mat learned from Dr. Murphy and Dr. Witherspoon that the man's condition was grave.[10]

Dr. Gally's medical background brought a few badly hurt men to his cabin seeking help. One of these, Augustus Schlieman, superintendent of the Erie Gold and Silver Mining Company and a man active in civic affairs in Austin, had gone to the Reveille district, southeast of Hot Creek. While there, in early January, he accidentally fired his shotgun as he pulled it out of the wagon. The muzzle was pointed in his direction and the shot lodged in his elbow. Wagner, his partner, brought him to Hot Creek to seek Dr. Gally's assistance in treating the wound.

Without proper medical instruments, there was little the doctor could do for Schlieman, although he considered improvising wire hooks and wood probes to clean out the wound. Instead, he dressed the wound as best he could and sent Schlieman on his way with words of encouragement. It took the injured man and his partner three-and-a-half days to reach Austin, and in that time, gangrene set in. Dr. Wixom, who attended him, noticed spasms and delayed amputating the arm; Schlieman died before anything could be done for him. There were people in Austin who criticized Dr. Gally for not taking more decisive action and for not removing the wads of clothing embedded in the "mass of torn muscle and fractured bones." Dr. Gally's reply to these criticisms was that "there is not a 'physician' at Hot Creek—not a drug store—not any surgical instruments—not even a butcher's meatsaw—not a place fit for a sick man." What more could he do than he had done? "Was it for us to tell him he would die?" With humility he declared: "Let those who are wiser do better when the time comes."[11]

Although Hot Creek was a great improvement over Roberts Creek, Mat and the children still had to fend for themselves while the doctor was away hauling ore from Morey and Reveille to Austin. Dr. Gally had turned to freighting to make ends meet while waiting for Eastern capitalists to become interested in the mines. Mat planted a garden and tended the vegetables and greens, which included onions, beets, and peas, and later lima beans, lettuce, radishes, corn, tomatoes, and parsnips. Mother and daughter found wildflowers and transplanted them in front of the cabin. They looked after the chickens, but did not have much luck with them during the first spring at Hot Creek. When their hen, Morisey, laid eggs early in

May, pig Tom worked his way into the hen house and made a supper of the eggs. A hawk preyed upon the chickens, and Mat asked one of the men to kill it. The rifle shots, however, went wide of the mark. Matters also went poorly with pig Betsey's litter, all of which was lost. The cat and her kittens fared as badly as the other domestic animals, becoming the victims of coyotes.

During the doctor's freighting trips to Austin, the days seemed unending. Over and over, Mat wrote of her loneliness and isolation: "lonely day," "very lonesome," "town dull and days long," "the days are long and lonesome," "long long weary day," "town dull & everything lonesome," and "a long gloomy day." Small accomplishments compensated for her feeling of loneliness. Mat recorded on May 18 that "we finished the Virginians" and on May 19 that she "read two acts in King Lear to the children."

Every so often there were other diversions to break the monotony. In one such instance, the fire under the kettle, which had not been entirely extinguished by the squaw who was helping Mat, was suddenly whipped up by a hot, dry wind. Had it not been noticed in time, it would have caused a conflagration. Lizards, scorpions, and rattlesnakes infested the area and created excitement from time to time. At the beginning of May, Matty discovered a strange-looking creature behind the stove, an animal her mother described as a cross between a lizard and a snake. Mat dislodged it, but the creature took cover under a log. She called a man for help, and he caught it with pincers and killed it. A more pleasant happening on May 22 was the arrival of 800 horses in the valley on their way to the states. It was exciting to watch the Mexican vaqueros do their work. Mat was seeing for the first time vaqueros "lasso, choke down, blind mount etc., just as I have often read of—the horses too 'bucked' in real Spanish fashion."

The usual chores seemed hardly enough to keep Mat from brooding. To pass the time, she sewed and performed several neighborly acts: a visit to a sick man; a tablecloth hemmed and a shirt altered for Mr. Gerow; and a shirt and towels washed and ironed for the same man, who insisted on paying her $1.50. Mat described her reaction to the money as "the first money I ever took in my life & I was as ashamed as a dog."[12] For a change now and then, she and the children walked up the canyon.

All of Mat's efforts to keep busy did not quiet her forebodings. She worried constantly about the doctor when he was away on trips and anxiously awaited word of his whereabouts from teamsters passing through Hot Creek. These men, noticing her anxiety, would reassure her that the doctor was safe and making progress on the road. As he started on one of his trips, on May 24, she wrote: "I wish we could have the Dr at home more." When they expected him home, Mat and the children would walk down the road, hoping to catch sight of him, but they often would return disappointed. His arrival safe and sound made them all happy.

On one occasion, Mat's uneasiness about Dr. Gally was not unfounded. A week after his departure for Austin in June, a number of smallpox cases were reported at Hot Creek, and the doctor's friend Rocky was rumored to be among the sick. Mat's anxiety about the doctor was not allayed until she received a note saying he was homeward bound. A day later, she learned that he had lost one of his horses at Clipper Gap Well; had been taken by Mr. Hinkle, the Hot Creek blacksmith, to the Stonebarger ranch; but had returned in the morning with two Indians to look for the horse again. Mat's informant did not know how he had made out. The apparent futility of their uncertain existence made her depressed, and she struggled to overcome the sense of defeat. "I have," she recorded on June 17, "to scold myself vigorously, & fortify myself with all the reason & strength at my command, to prevent total discouragement." For all her worrying, the doctor found his horse, Punch, and Rocky was soon on his feet and paying them a visit.

Between trips, the doctor was busy preparing for his next expedition. It was not unusual for him to spend the first day after his arrival home reading in bed, but the second day he was up spading in the garden or working on the wagon. The wagon, which was essential for making a living, needed constant overhauling. The wheels required frequent tightening and various parts, such as the tongue, had to be replaced or mended. The job of tightening the spindles was exacting and time-consuming. When Mat helped with the work, she found herself tired out at night and suffering from a strained back. The doctor kept doggedly at the task until he had finished, however, and the quiet determination he maintained in facing frustration led Mat to observe that "I could have cried with sorrow at his troubles which he bore so patiently."[13]

The care and safety of the horses caused as much anxiety as the wagon. The doctor permitted them to graze freely at night, but he refused to continue on a trip until he had found all of his horses, which sometimes held him up for days at a time. A real blow came at the end of July when the doctor found Jule dead on the flat from no immediate apparent cause. The horse's death made him feel "anxious and uncomfortable."[14]

* * *

Dr. Gally's work took him along the byroads to Austin from the distant outlying camps. Between January and August, he made several major trips from Reveille to Austin, as well as one to the Roberts Creek ranch. By mid-June, he was thoroughly acquainted with mining conditions in the southeastern country, and when he arrived in Austin with a wagonload of ore from Reveille, he gave a glowing report of the region to the local newspaper. For almost 200 miles from Reese River to Pahranagat, mineral belts had been discovered.

A large number of wagons were carrying ore from Reveille to Austin; the entire line of camps along the Hot Creek and Reveille ranges lacked a first-rate mill to work the ore. At Morey, they were reducing a few tons of ore with an arrastra, and at Hot Creek, the mill of the Consolidation Company was idle awaiting the installation of roasting furnaces. Until the relative worth of these districts could be established, heavy freight charges had to be incurred by prospectors.[15]

Despite the many miles tramped by prospectors and teamsters, the region southeast of Hot Creek and Reveille and beyond was little known even in Nevada. It was thought of as a region "cheerless, trackless, treeless, waterless," and it was true that in winter, the land had its disagreeable features. The dawns of the winter mornings were bitterly cold, and the sharp wind "cut keenly, covering our faces with ice, and almost piercing the very marrow in our bones," according to Mahlon D. Fairchild. To the initiated, however, the country also had a pleasant side. In the spring and summer, blue joint grass covered the valley floors and the undulating hills. Springs abounded whose waters were delectably cool on a hot day, and wide-ranging growths of trees covered the slopes.[16]

The pattern of travel for Dr. Gally and his fellow teamsters was regulated by the number of daylight hours and the availability of water. Up at dawn, they would make a sagebrush fire over which to cook the bacon and heat the water for coffee. Not far away, a coyote, scenting the frying bacon, might howl with hunger. Once breakfast was finished, the blankets were rolled up, and the search for the horses began. If they were all near the camping site, the travelers were ready to begin. But a stray horse who had snapped his hobble straps might hold up the march for an entire day or more, as the hapless teamster tramped the hills looking for him. If he could not find the horse, the owner would desert his wagon and hurry to the nearest mining camp to recruit an Indian with whom he could return to continue the search. The loss of a horse was a serious misfortune, and a man with no horse and without other conveyance, "walks weary days and sleeps tired nights, from water to water, until, at length, he trudges into a mining camp, foot sore, aching and dusty."[17] But if all went well, the day's journey began without mishap over the sagebrush valley and the alkali flats.

In his story "Big Jack Small," Dr. Gally depicted vividly the work of the Nevada teamster. An encounter with heavy mud on one of the alkali flats meant hard pulling for oxen and horses, and when the wagon sank to its hubs, double teaming or unloading was necessary to free the wagon. Over an ungraded road to a new camp like Reveille, all kinds of mishaps were possible. The doctor described the difficulty in steadying the large, ox-drawn freighters' wagons when they struck the downgrade of an uneven stretch and began "to reel to and fro like boats at sea." Even a wagon expertly handled could topple on the edge of a "shallow, dry water-wash." Days were passed struggling over the valley floor or ascending laboriously "slowly—ah, so slowly, so dustily! up and up the mountain by the canyon road, pausing at intervals to breath the panting herd."

The stop for supper and the night brought relief to tired bone and muscle. The aroma of sizzling bacon and steaming coffee meant that supper was on its way. The bacon and coffee neutralized the effect of the alkali dust breathed during the day's journey. In the embers of the fire, bread for the next day was made. Then it was time for a smoke as night followed dusk. Off in the distance, the howling of a coyote disturbed the silence and contrasted sharply with the sound of the whippoorwill and other birds in the Eastern woodlands.

By the fire, the solitary man was a mere speck in nature's vast domain. "The bright moon and stars," observed Dr. Gally, "moved on their long-appointed courses through the wide and cloudless sky, the sagebrush of the valley stretched far away, the mountain rose ragged to the serrated summit, the cattle browsed along the slope, the shadows of the great wagons fell square and dark upon the dry desert earth, and nature's old, old silence closed down upon the wilderness." On a clear night, such as that described by the doctor, the bedding was spread out on the ground. In inclement weather, the bedding was spread under the wagon, and a teamster would roll up in his blankets for the night.

Often, the teamster took along with him a denizen of

the sagebrush, a Paiute or Shoshone Indian, to help gather firewood and bring up the horses or oxen in the morning. An Indian serving in this capacity, with a nickname like "Gov Nye," usually was attired in a colorful assortment of cast-off white men's clothing. One of Dr. Gally's Indians wore "a battered, black-silk 'plug' hat, a corporal's military coat with chevrons on the sleeves and buttoned to the chin, a pair of red drawers for pantaloons, a red blanket hanging gracefully from his arm, and a pair of dilapidated boots on his feet." Sometimes, a few Indians would wander into the evening bivouac, hoping to enjoy a morsel of the white man's meal, preferring it to their own meager diet of "lizards and mice, grass seeds, thistle roots, pismire's eggs." Half-starved, they unceremoniously devoured the grease in the frying pan or, if opportunity permitted, stole off with a slab of bacon.

For weeks at a time in every season, teamsters like the doctor plodded along, with the sagebrush waste and solitude offering opportunity for contemplation. Men's minds became attuned to the finer subtleties of the senses, an education that begins with nature itself. To the untutored eye, the landscape of Nevada is merely a gray monotone, unrelieved by brilliant contrasts of color. But once the eye perceives the terrain, the discovery is made that nowhere else "does Nature paint with a touch so delicate or a spirit so masterful." Upon the face of the land are reflected—in the absence of atmospheric interference—"the shadows painted by the sun, the moon, or the stars." Dr. Gally was prone to examine the immensity of nature's work, and he saw the universe in the light of a grand "Gothic spirituality." His character, "Big Jack Small," a teamster like himself, expresses the doctor's conviction:

"Well, I don't know! Seems to me thar was never
nothin' born in Judear that hed hands that kin lay over
Ameriky—an' nothin' was never born in Ameriky that
hed hands that kin build a ten-cent sideshow fer that ar
canyon! Parson, them's things that can't be wiped out,
nor wrong printed in no book!—nor no new light can't
make 'em more'n they jest are! Whatever made sech
things as them, an' these yere mountains, that's my God.
But He hain't got no hands in the image o' these yere!"
extending his thorny, blackened palms, and adding as a
climax, "ye kin bet yer sweet life on that."[18]

The doctor was busy freighting into the summer, but
by the middle of July he had completed the last job. While
returning from Austin, the wheels of the wagon broke the
back of the Gallys' dog, Ring, and he had to be killed.
"Alas! poor Ring!" wrote Mat. Nevertheless, the doctor's
arrival home on Friday, July 19, was a happy event, and
Mat's morale was bolstered when she learned that he
would not be immediately on the road again. For one
thing, his appointment as justice of the peace for Hot
Creek obligated him to stay close to home. A new
business venture of manufacturing adobes for the mill and
other parties consumed his time in the months ahead. By
the middle of the year, the Gallys had secured a foothold
in the new settlement, and although they had not become
rich, the future did not look bad.

The Gallys could take comfort in the thriving
condition of the camp. One indication of prosperity was
the activity at the Old Dominion Mill, which had
commenced working ore on September 2. The mill netted
$8,060 in ten days. Two of the doctor's mines, the
"Henry Clay" and the "Leviathan," had been put in the
hands of I. T. Irwin for sale in the Eastern market. Much
was expected from this move, though Mat could not have

helped recalling the great expectations surrounding the disastrous South Humboldt speculation.

* * *

The second half of the year passed rapidly. The doctor completed more work on the house, daubing the room, topping out the chimney, and building a bedstead and bunks for the children. Feeling more secure about the future, the doctor was in a happier frame of mind. He became more of a companion to Jimmy, who was nearing his eleventh birthday, taking him along in the wagon to Rattlesnake Canyon and asking him to assist in hauling a wagonload of logs. The doctor realized that the boy had never enjoyed robust health, but he treated him as if he did.

In December, Dr. Gally took Jimmy prospecting with him, and they camped out, sleeping in the tent. The boy enjoyed this kind of outing, even though he came home dirty and tired and had to be promptly washed and sent to bed. Matty was not taken along on these trips, but she had enough activities and interests to occupy her time. She cared for her pony's newborn colt, brought him through the weaning stage, and with Jimmy's assistance, broke him for riding. Early in December, she found a sick calf that had fallen out of a herd of cattle passing through the valley. She fed it and kept diligent watch over it, but her efforts were in vain: the calf died within a few days. A week later she again was disappointed when the black pig gave stillbirth to two pigs, although earlier one of their pigs had delivered a litter of seven.

The entire family had a settled-down feeling by autumn, although they still had to contend with the daily problems of frontier living. The hawks, coyotes, and wolves, for example, were bothersome. During the last week of October, the wolves and coyotes laid siege to the chicken house, making off with fifteen or sixteen of the fowl. The doctor poisoned five coyotes in two nights, Mat poisoned two, and Mr. Dillmer, a close neighbor, took a shot at one that was lurking in the rear of the house in the middle of November. "The wolves carried off nearly all my chickens a month ago," Mat recorded on December 25, "so no turkey dinner."

Catastrophe
and Decline

Mining camps taught hard lessons, and Hot Creek was no exception. At the beginning of 1868, there were signs that the camp was in trouble. The miners could talk about rich ledges, but mining activity had ground to a halt. On January 13, Mat wrote, "No mill at work today for want of quartz," and on January 18 she observed, "The Sierras are blockaded with snow so as to make it difficult to procure freight from Virginia City." Many were waiting to pack up and leave, but the deep snow and bitter cold made travel dangerous if not impossible.

Snow in the Sierra had cut off travel between California and Nevada; freight shipments from Virginia City were halted; and horse teams were not leaving Austin for the southeast, although a few teams of oxen were attempting to stay on the road. When the Gallys looked out their door on the morning of January 20, there were ten inches of snow on the ground and more was falling. "The storm begins to look serious," observed Mat, and she could remember nothing like it since the winter in Iowa. All during the remaining days of January the cold hung on, letting up only briefly for a fresh fall of snow. Even the water and meat stored in the house froze solid. Looking out on the stark white expanse framed by a clear moonlit night, Mat saw a first-quarter moon that offered a "remarkable spectacle of being attended by two evening stars Venus and Mercury—to which phenomenon the wise men attribute our stormy weather."[1]

Snowed in, the Gallys had to attend to their own immediate needs. They insulated the main living area of the house as best they could, but as Mat noted they had "just as much as we can do to keep warm, we burn one side & freeze the other. . . . We hung up the tent in the open space between the rooms."[2] The doctor fetched the wood, which could be obtained only at a distance. After several hours of exposure to the cold on January 23, he returned chilled to the bone, and while eating his dinner he complained of severe pains in the side. Mat thought he had strained himself and she "used chloroform inside & out & in an hour or two he was easier."

There were too many matters requiring Dr. Gally's attention for him to remain in bed. The logs for the fire were frozen together, and the doctor and Jimmy had to separate them by blasting and chopping. He struggled to keep alive a newborn piglet, which refused to take warm milk from a bowl. "The Dr.," recorded Mat, "fitted a glove finger with a sponge tied it on to the bottle containing the milk & piggy thinks it is his mother."[3] In spite of the care, the piglet died. There was no flour or sugar in Joslyn's store, and the doctor had to walk the length of the camp to find a small quantity of sugar to sweeten the children's food.

The Gallys devised entertainment for themselves, resorting to those pursuits they had always enjoyed most. The doctor read from the *Vestiges of Creation* and the *Merchant of Venice*. The former work was absorbing to Mat and she felt she had "received much solid information that I have long desired."[4] Mat also was interested in the recognition given to Dickens, and she recorded on January 19 that "the papers are full of Dickens—so far his readings appear to have been perfectly successful." The reading of the *Merchant of Venice* was a concession to the children, whose exposure to Shakespeare was already great and who clamored to have this particular play reread. When not reading to them, the doctor encouraged the children to keep busy. For example, he had Matty assist him in making a pair of overshoes from Brussels carpet material. The children's studies were not overlooked, and Jimmy had progressed to fractions, while Matty was beginning simple multiplication.

Enforced idleness gave Mat and the doctor a chance to complete a few special projects. Dr. Gally made a robe of wildcat skins, and Mat caught up on her sewing. As Mat explained, "I finished a new vest for the Dr which I cut out of an old coat the vest looks quite well but I am in a sad dilemma for lack of buttons—these little out of the way camps very inconvenient."[5] Although the family members made the best of a bad situation, they were not able to overcome the aching sense of complete isolation. The feelings of depression which had overwhelmed Mat two years before at the Roberts Creek ranch gripped her again. Most of the days seemed "long sad and lonesome."

Besides the bad weather and the unending isolation,

the family caused her concern. The children were not well and suffered from colds and bad coughs. Trying to dry out their lungs in the drafty cabin in which they were forced to move around to stay warm was impossible. Mat's concern about the children was heightened when Matty, who was aged ten, suddenly became hysterical:

> Matty was attacked with a violent nervous headache, accompanied by what was unusual in such a child, stron[g] symptoms of hysteria—shivering gasping sobbing fainting chilliness choking etc.—I used the best remedies at my command & had succeeded in partially alleviating the pain & producing quiet before her Father came but was more than relieved to see him coming over the hill. Matty was constantly wishing for him too—he used brandy & chloroform & she after a while dozed & now after several wakings & partial relapses is sleeping.[6]

Bad news from the East did not help matters. A letter from the doctor's sister, Margaret, informed them that his mother was dying. Three weeks later another letter, received on February 1, told them that the old woman had died on January 1. She was eighty years old and Mat declared:

> We of course knew she must soon go "over the river"—still we feel badly & even at this distance miss her sadly—a better truer woman never lived—she possessed great judgment & endurance—warm and patient affection & through a long & chequered life bore herself thoroughly honestly & with the most womanly modesty & courage.[7]

The doctor's problems were overshadowed by another event. Early in January, a small stamp mill had commenced operations, but this mill and the Old Dominion mill ceased operating with the coming of cold weather. The worst possible misfortune happened when the larger of the two mills, the Old Dominion, caught fire on the night of February 4 and burned to the ground. The fire started as men worked to thaw out a water pipe leading into the mill by igniting rubbish beneath the engine room. The flames, as described by one spectator, appeared "to dance like fiends among the shadows of the great rocks."[8]

The fire at the Old Dominion mill, which had been adequate to work the ore of the Hot Creek mines and of the surrounding districts, wiped out a major economic resource for the area. The men at the mill were without work and were unable to collect their wages; those who held bills against the mill owners had worthless paper. "This last misfortune," sighed Mat, "will I suppose ruin this camp, at least temporarily."[9]

Every possibility for the camp's future was considered. One of the owners of the Old Dominion, Mr. Montgomery, came to Hot Creek in the second week of February, and he spoke of promptly restoring the mill. This piece of news bolstered the courage of the mine owners, who believed that the mines still could produce high-quality ore. Another good sign appeared after the bitter cold snap in January. Work in the mines resumed, and two miners, Robinson and Walters, had begun to bring out good-paying rock from the Pioneer and Philadelphia mines. Most of the Hot Creek people were banking on the mines to keep the camp from disintegrating. "There seems," observed Mat, "to be a more hopeful feeling abroad in the camp—they have fine specimens from the new ledges."[10]

There was nothing to do but wait, and spring seemed slow in coming. February had brought more snow and cold as well as hardships and suffering. Two Reveille men were trapped by the elements; one of them died from overexposure and the other's limbs were amputated because of gangrene. As for the Gallys, the lack of sunshine had made them all sick. Mat caught the children's colds and for several days felt badly, noting that "my throat is very sore—the uvula so inflamed & elongated as to make every breath an annoyance."[11] The cold blustery March weather made matters worse. One night was so cold that the water in the back room froze to a thickness of one-half inch; and Matty, who still had a cold, was packed in heated bricks. Mat slept in snatches while the wind howled throughout the night.

The Gallys felt depressed, and perhaps in keeping with their mood, they took a walk "to see the 'graveyard'" above the house. More constructively, they tried to break the monotony of the usual routine. The children and the doctor took their turns at cooking; the doctor made a "chili colorado stew," while Jimmy helped with the baking and Matty helped with a stew. Mat accompanied the doctor in the wagon on some of his forays into the surrounding country in search of wood. In the evening, she read from Shakespeare and reread with great enjoyment a neighbor's copy of Bulwer's *My Novel*.

The family was thankful for small favors. A fierce March storm, which piled up five-foot drifts on the western slopes of the Hot Creek Range, did not reach Hot Creek Valley. The Hot Creek settlement was again receiving groceries and foodstuffs from Austin, and the doctor stockpiled flour and replenished the larder with several other staple commodities. On March 17, they were cheered by the warmth of the sun's direct rays; leaving the cold cabin, mother and daughter took a long walk under the clear blue sky to warm up. A week later there was more snow on the ground, but the spring sun melted it quickly and brought clear skies. The wet hills, warmed by the sun's rays, were covered with green grass; everywhere the sounds of spring were heard from the arriving flocks of bluebirds and the croaking frogs. "The bluebirds," exclaimed Mat, "have come in quantities. God grant they may betoken a pleasant & early spring." [12]

Everyone's health improved, as did the humor of the inhabitants of the camp. Some of the neighboring families made long visits, and the Gally children played ball with the Smythe youngsters. The Gally children's favorite adult friends came with gifts hand-fashioned especially for them: a small toy wagon from Mr. Rosine and a boat for Jimmy from Mr. Tipton. Even the doctor presented the children with two small boats and a dancing man that he had made. He and Mr. Tipton also took time to construct a swing for them.

Activity was evident in the settlement, which encouraged everyone. The pack trains were moving over the road from Austin, and on March 27, one outfit arrived in Hot Creek with a supply of flour. The early spring revival was more in the minds of people than a reality, however. Mr. Smythe lost a mortgage on a property, and other disconcerting events followed. It had become clear that the Old Dominion mill would not be rebuilt immediately and that the trustees of the Old Dominion Silver Mining Company had been stalling. The mining company was heavily in debt to everyone, and an ugly mood in the settlement forced Dr. Gally's constable to resign his position. The tension was great as the sheriff began to attach property shortly after midnight on April 6. A suit was brought against the Old Dominion Silver

Mining Company, and the mines themselves were drawn into the collapse.[13]

The collapse of the Old Dominion mining enterprise was an irreparable blow. A new mill, which would be large enough to handle the ore of the district, was essential for the survival of the Hot Creek settlement. The failure to have such a mill had bankrupted the camp. But on April 3, Mat noted that "there seems to be more hope in the camp today, some whisper of M & M putting up a brick mill."

The optimism and well-being of April 3 soon vanished, however. Mat wrote on April 5: "M & M both here & the Company is a perfect crash. The camp has nothing to hope for in regard to this Company, but the mines look well." The Gallys were discouraged, and Mat complained that "my throat sore & I feel miserably in mind as well as body."[14] Almost every day brought either wind, snow, rain, or hail, which prompted Mat to say that they were having the "most miserable weather only equaled in gloom by the hopelessness of the camp. I have done nothing all day."[15]

Mat seemed to be confronted with nothing but new frustrations. Their pig, Suse, turned up with a large section of her flank ripped off, and Mat was at a loss to know how it had happened. The animal was almost ready to give birth to piglets, and Mat was worried about the outcome. She vented her irritation on the doctor and believed that had he not been in Belmont, he "could I think sew up the wound."[16] She could not obtain any groceries from the nearly defunct store and was lucky to be able to pick up a can of sardines there. They were reduced to eating bread, coffee, onions, and molasses for their evening meal and very similar fare for breakfast.

Suppers of codfish balls, an oyster stew, a baked ham, or just plain salmon were relished as treats. Seeking some variety in their meals, Mat went out to gather greens, and was disappointed that the "'lambs quarter' was small."[17]

Everything about the camp seemed hopeless; many of the neighbors were packing up and departing. The blacksmith shop was dismantled and moved to a more prosperous locality. The collapse of business in the camp made life even more gloomy for the Hot Creek people, and Mat noted this feeling of oppression: "The camp is very dull nothing in the stores and no money to buy if there was."[18]

Dr. Gally and the children saw Mat's disillusionment and unhappiness and tried to cheer her up. The doctor took a good look at Suse and reassured Mat that the animal would recover and would give birth to a healthy litter. He was right; several days later Suse had two piglets. In addition, the doctor made a special effort to be congenial. He found a rocking chair in Morey and carried it the fifteen miles to Hot Creek. "I wondered he had patience to carry it," declared Mat.[19]

The diligence of the children set an example for everyone. Jimmy spent one day combing through the burned-out mill for nails. Both he and Matty worked hard to throw up a dirt embankment to keep the water in the brickyard from overflowing into the pig's pit. Another couple of days were spent putting the brickyard in order. Matty rose before the others one morning to ride out on her pony in search of the horses, which were needed for an excursion to gather wood. She also pleased her mother by small attentions. As soon as the first spring flowers were up, the girl gathered some and had "two brilliant bunches decorating the window but they are entirely devoid of fragrance."[20]

For all their goodness, the children were a source of anxiety for Mat. When Jimmy started out for Upper Town in search of their pigs, he was attacked in the canyon by a dog belonging to Mrs. Wiggins. The boy arrived home with a ripped jacket, and he was badly frightened. His mother observed that "his very lips were white & he trembled still."[21] The next day she inspected his clothes and body more closely, discovering that the "dog bit through James' thick heavy jacket, two flannel shirts & even bruised the flesh though not I think breaking the skin—the dog should be killed."[22] But Mat did not take up the matter with Mrs. Wiggins, possibly because this neighbor was extremely worried about her little nephew, who was at the time suffering from a high fever. Other dogs in the vicinity were as troublesome as that of Mrs. Wiggins. A dog belonging to Mr. Page was the bane of Mat's pig, Suse, and inflicted upon her some ugly wounds.

While Mat was worrying about the dogs, a miner named Pete Cunningham fell and broke his ankle while working in the Gillett shaft. The night before the accident, Mr. Gillett had carelessly thrown the rope around the windlass, planning to anchor it properly the next day. Unaware of this situation, Cunningham seized the rope, swung himself into the shaft, and was hurled to the bottom. "It was of course unintentional (the arrangement of the rope)," declared Mat, "but horribly, & it appears fatally careless."[23] At first, there appeared to be cause to hope for the man's life. Dr. Dehl and Dr. Cummings were summoned from Belmont to set the fracture, and the day after their arrival, Cunningham felt somewhat better. Within a week, however, he declined rapidly, having suffered more serious internal injuries than could be treated by the medical knowledge of the day.

The sick man lingered on for almost three weeks. Mr. Johnston, the butcher, looked after him, but in caring for Cunningham's injured leg, he developed an infection in his own hand. The long days of waiting as Pete Cunningham died left an indelible impression upon the doctor's memory. With the name changed and a few other details altered, he wrote movingly of the scene:

> Strange, strong men were there, going in and out, and the big nails in their heavy boots made queer pictures in the dust of the dirt-floor; but there was no noise, no useless, fussy moving about—only quiet, patient attention. They had kept constant guard over him for two nights, with that aching suspense that waits, not knowing what better to do, and watches wounded life, and listens for the Doctor's wheels among the echoing aisles of mountain crags.
>
> As the Doctor went forward and bent over Dan's prostrate body, the men formed unconsciously a new circle behind him—their heads only a few inches from the low roof—and looked and listened, each chest heaving with silent, suppressed breathing, until the Doctor said,
>
> "There is not enough air in this place."
>
> Then instantly and quietly each man left the little room to stand outside and whisper, or gaze reflectively down the bank upon the willows in the canyon, until the Doctor came out. No one asked any questions; but, as the Doctor looked in the face of each and then shook his head in the face of all, they knew for certain that which they nearly knew before. Crowder did not come out; but I, as in some degree his backer in this case, went immediately in and found Dan's old pard sitting by his bedside, upon one of those clumsy wooden stools so common in mining camps. We were silent for some moments, when Dan, poor fellow, as stoutly and cheerily

as he could, said,

"Boys, my driving power is a total wreck. I'll never get up steam again."

Nobody responded. Nobody knew any true word suitable for response, and death will not accept a flattery.[24]

* * *

As gloomy as matters had been during the spring months, the Gallys grasped at every new straw that promised a future for the camp. The discoveries of a new ledge at Hot Creek and rich leads in the Rattlesnake area a few miles to the south were heartening. In fact, the discoveries had brought in New York capitalists whose presence led to renewed hope about the building of a new mill—possibly across the canyon from the Gally homestead. There was also a glowing report from Judge Ferris, who had spoken to a mining expert and had come away satisfied that Hot Creek will be "one of the richest districts in the state."[25]

During the latter part of the spring and until autumn, there was some small basis for belief in the immediate future of the Hot Creek mines. Operations began in mid-May on several new mines, and the Gillett mine, yielding "rock with great lumps of native silver,"[26] aroused hope. A small mill commenced operations at the end of June, but in a few weeks it was nearly bankrupt. The Old Dominion was being rebuilt by Miller in Upper Town and was operating by the summer. Toward the end of the year, Gillett, the mine owner, had a small mill processing ore for a few weeks.

These few bright rays hardly transformed the nature

of life for the Gallys. The daily struggle was as stern as it had always been. In May, Mat could see for herself the reflection of depressed mining conditions in the faces of discouraged men "who had walked from Los Angeles to Pahranagat arrived there just as the mills all closed & were compelled to beg their way while hunting for work."[27]

The almost complete lack of flour in central and eastern Nevada was one example of the misfortune the Hot Creek residents shared. On June 11, Mat recorded in her diary: "There is no flour for sale in Austin, none in Belmont—families being without even corn bread for days. We have about 75 pds more perhaps than anyone else in camp—no flour from below to come up—it looks like starvation." Neighbors borrowed bucketfuls of flour from one another, and many people had not eaten bread for weeks. The Hot Creek boardinghouse was serving a monotonous diet of beans and coffee. Mat commented that "we have still some flour & mill, more fortunate than our neighbors who are eating beans and barley."[28] By July 10, the Gallys had consumed all of their flour—both begged and bought—and Mat was boiling beans and pearled barley. To satisfy voracious appetites with this kind of fare, however, was impossible. The doctor rode the several miles to Rattlesnake Canyon to obtain a few pounds of flour, and three days later a large supply of provisions came in. The Gallys were then able to buy flour, butter, bacon, and fish at Joslyn's Hot Creek store. The flour shortage had lasted an entire month during a season when supplies could readily be moved over the roads. In September, there would be new shortages at Hot Creek, although flour could be obtained in Belmont. Butter, soap, and other basic staples became less available as the camp declined. Toward the end of October, Mat lamented: "No flour for sale in town & we are almost out. Such a country."[29]

In addition to shortages of the staple items of food, there were many kinds of minor personal irritations. Whenever a strong wind blew down the canyon, the clothes hanging on the line were likely to be covered with a yellow dust. The cold, wintry weather extended late into May, aggravating the feelings of depression. Mat's mood was recorded in her diary for May 21: "Most wretched weather—snowed and hailed this morning; rained and hailed this afternoon. No adjectives vile enough to fitly describe such weather. And today they say we have a new moon which for[e]tells (they say) a month of such misery." A warm day or two brought out the mosquitoes and gnats, which were extremely annoying. Mat also suffered more than the other members of the family from intermittent sore throat, headache, cramps, and aching teeth and jaw. She swabbed her throat and gums with caustic, applied mustard poultices to her neck, and took chloroform for general malaise.

As bad as the situation was, the Gallys did not want to give up at Hot Creek. Everything now depended upon the outcome of work on the Gillett ledge in Hot Creek Canyon and on the Raymond Company ledges in Rattlesnake Canyon. In a few months, the value of these new mines would be known. Meanwhile, those miners who were not working needed to find employment. After a winter of stagnation, many of the Hot Creek people turned their attention to farming.

Dr. Gally had arranged with a friend, Mr. Tipton, to clear some irrigable land in Six Mile Canyon, which was located several miles north of Hot Creek. Jimmy went with the men, and although Mat missed "James' pale face much," there was no need for worry. She had been told by the doctor that the boy was enjoying the change.[30] Two days later she wrote:

> Last evening the clouds thickened until the dashing showers became a continuous driving rain & the night most intensely dark—after midnight the wind rose & the rain seemed blown away. I spent an anxious uncomfortable night both my boys away! the Dr with not even a blanket. I sat up until nearly morning kept a big fire before which hung a warm dry change of clothing for the Dr if he should unfortunately come.

Mat and Matty made the best of life in the absence of Jimmy and Dr. Gally. Matty scurried over the hillsides that were blooming with flowers, and Mat fretted about the miserable quality of the bread she had made with borrowed yeast. She decided to prepare "sweet light yeast of my own manufacture, which will give me good bread tomorrow. Nothing vexes me as much as bad bread."[31]

Mat continued to be concerned about Jimmy, or James, as he now was called. He was almost twelve years old, but his mother was having a difficult time accepting his bid for independence. On one of his trips home, she noted that he was tired and tongue-in-cheek declared "he misses his 'mommy' I guess."[32] When the men sent him home in the rain for some equipment, Mat decided that the meager protection provided by Tipton's borrowed coat was not adequate; immediately she had him put on a rubber coat and pants. After eight days of separation from the boy, Mat vented her feelings about the trials he had suffered as a result of the cold, wind, and rain, as well as the inadequate fare he was eating, but her real complaints were quite visible. "James," she wrote, "has never but once before been away from me so long—the spring that Mother died I went with her to Ky and stayed ten days leaving Jimmy at home with his Father and Aunties."[33]

She worried needlessly about James, however, for he stood up well under the elements. Miserable weather—snow, rain, and hail—was almost a daily occurrence. The men and James persisted in the work at the ranch; by the third week of May, they had planted the potato cuttings and had put in lettuce, radishes, and cabbage.

Work at the ranch was temporarily interrupted by more pressing matters. The Gallys' hogs had to be driven from the Hot Creek Canyon, where they were trampling the gardens, to springs seven miles away from the homestead. The entire family went on the outing, with the doctor on foot scouting for a good foraging area and Mat driving the wagon. Since it was late by the time they reached the springs, they had supper and improvised a tent by turning the wagon box on its side and covering it with a tarpaulin. The arrangement worked well enough, although the mosquitoes kept Mat and Matty awake.

During May and June, the family made several trips to prepare beds for seeding the cantaloupe, squash, lettuce, peas, beets, turnips, and parsnip seeds. In late June, on their way to the ranch, they had trouble with their horse, Punch:

> After a tedious march we dropped the hogs & went on for the ranche—it was quite dark by the time we began to cross the creek but we got on finely until the last crossing which was an ugly one because of a steep, loose stony pitch down to the water & the dense growth of the willows. The children went over on their horses; we got safely down the pitch when just as we entered the water Punch laid flat down. By this time it was quite dark, the water roaring and the willows in a perfect tangle. Punch

floundered round in the water, got her body under the tongue of the wagon—her head in the willow roots, came near breaking Beck's legs & drowning herself—this she did in her effort to get up. The Dr jumped into the water knee deep, got Beck loose & tied to a bush, & then we by a tremendous effort braced the wagon—hitched Beck to her pulled her head out of the water & got off the harness. Now there was nothing to prevent her getting up but either through fear or stubbornness she would not try. The Dr exhausted whips & willows at length struck her with the stay chain. This mode of treatment induced her to get up & walk off. We were obliged to camp there & were thankful to get off as well as we did.[34]

Trips to the ranch in July had almost an idyllic quality. Nights during the early part of the month were beautiful. On one evening, in the light of the moon, the doctor and Mat watered the crops until midnight, while James and Matty slumbered "sweetly." By now, the heads of lettuce were sufficiently large for the table and the other plants were doing well. On one evening, Mat sat by a blazing fire awaiting the return of her husband, who had spent the day climbing a peak to the east of the canyon. What she thought was the bleating of sheep, turned out to be the echoing footsteps of the doctor, who came in with a bundle of assorted rock and wood. "After they were all in bed," wrote Mat, "I sat by the fire, watched the shadows & lights as the moon came over the hill, & then turned in."[35]

By August they were bringing home more lettuce, as well as turnips, beets and beans; and the doctor made a special trip to gather potatoes that he wanted to sell in the local market. The most likely danger to the crops in late August and early September was a premature frost, a fear which was soon realized. As they were on the way to the

ranch on September 1, they met Tipton who exclaimed:
"The frost has slayed us." The situation was not as bad
as he described it, however, and while a few plants were
damaged, most of them merely needed water. The
problem now was to obtain a fresh supply of water from
the creek, which required digging a new ditch and two
dams.

The corn was nearly ready to be picked, but the
doctor began another trip to the White Pine Mining
District. Mat explained the reason for the trip in her diary
entry of September 14:

> I feel with the old astronomer 'And still she moves'! . . .
> the Raymond Co. have stopped work as their is no
> money—through Mr. D says Garrett & Joslyn have rec'd
> letter from Mr. Gager stating the nonarrival of funds is
> caused by the reception of letters (on the part of the
> Company in N.Y.) written by some person in Hot Creek
> saying that these mines are & always have been a "bilk"
> etc—much indignation is expressed by the men. I think
> there is very little hope for the prosperity of the camp.

When the doctor had not returned after two weeks,
Mat was worried: "I am too vexed to think of the corn all
drying up at the ranche & we getting none of it."[36] In
desperation, on October 1, she hitched up the horses and
drove with the children to the ranch. "I felt," she noted,
"considerable anxiety in making such a drive, but there
was nothing else to do. The children drove well & were as
good as they could be." She had not come out any too
soon, as her diary entry for October 2 reveals:

> We found the upper garden very dry, the cabbage not
> heading rapidly & suffering from vermin. The lower
> garden was wet enough, but the ripest of the corn &
> melons had been pulled. There was a lot of horses

> making great havoc, completely destroying the corn. We drove them off but they will soon be back. The children dug some potatoes, a bag full. I gathered a dozen or so of the ripest melons, five or six dozen of corn, two or three squash, a few peas & beans, turnips, beets, etc. We turned off the water packed the wagon & got home without any trouble about 3 P.M.

Even with Mat's efforts, much of the Gallys' crop was destroyed. The horses in the canyon had trampled the corn and consumed the tops of the beets and carrots, while the aphids had devoured the cabbages. Mat recorded on November 11:

> I was miserably sick all night—the oxen got at the potatoes turned the hay about, knocked down the roof & stockades & I was kept constantly jumping up & running out in the cold—at last in desperation I drove them away below the fence in my night dress. I had a chill when I came back & was miserable enough all night.

In spite of the setbacks, they brought in several hundred pounds of potatoes and a hundred pounds of turnips, carrots, and beets at the end of October. For once, their perseverance had produced moderately successful results.

* * *

After the Gallys had expended so much energy and time at Hot Creek, they were almost desperate at the thought of losing everything. Mat courageously resisted this sense of panic. The doctor did not escape ridicule when he showed any sign of weakness, and Mat frowned upon his occasional retreat to bed without cause. She was hardly sympathetic to his complaints about ''two small boils on his corporation which he makes a great fuss about—has been on the lounge nearly all day and asleep this afternoon."[37] In contrast, she pitied James, who had a boil and who had "to lay down in the road, he was so miserable—his boil is swollen angry."[38]

Frontier life had left its imprint on Mat. She understood the dimension of patience in her life. Most important of all, she had learned to wait. "After sundown," she wrote, "I was sitting at the door waiting waiting to see the Dr coming down the road."[39] During those hours and days of waiting, she continually had to fight the anxiousness she had always felt on the frontier. When her patience wore thin, she would complain: "We have passed a dull stupid day."[40]

Mat was embittered most by the purposelessness of her life. "I hope," she wrote in July, "we will never spend another summer so undecided & aimless as this has been."[41] She liked to be busy, but she frequently found she had nothing to do. A sense of loneliness overwhelmed her at those times, and she missed the doctor. While he was away on a trip in September and Mat and the family had spent a dismally cold day, she wrote in her diary: "I do hope the Doctor is warm & comfortable. I do wish we could arrange to live so that he might be absent less frequently." The appearance of the doctor was like a tonic for Mat, and seeing him come up the road dissipated the "lonesome & worried & half sick" mood into which she sank when he was away. Through the struggles of the past few years, her essential affection for him had not diminished, and she once paid him a high compliment in her diary: "I guess my husband is the best husband in the country. God bless him."[42]

The poetic quality of Mat's spirit figured largely in

sustaining her strength. She easily found momentary loveliness that lifted her above the poverty of her own life. In the moon that ''rode above & through the clouds & shone clear & triumphant,'' she found a simile for her own will to survive. A Nevada sunset, for example, overpowered her with its beauty:

> For about an hour just after sunset the heavens were magnificent beyond description. The masses of cloud of infinite variety of shade and shape lying so grandly against or floating so lightly upon the clear pure bright blue of the sky lighted too by the gorgeous hues of the setting sun all combined to create a view whose rare beauty I can better appreciate than describe.[43]

Domesticity and Camp Life

Hot creek was dying in mid-1868. Most of the inhabitants lived poorly, and some of them were practically penniless. Dr. Gally described the effects of life in such camps on the inhabitants:

Between those camps which have become cities and those which have gone back into wilderness, there are others, which remain in *status quo*—which neither die, nor grow—objects of arrested development; but which are self-supporting, on a slender thread of rich ore, laboriously mined by a hopeful few, who believe that a bonanza must exist somewhere on its line as it penetrates the rocks—or else these hopeful few support their hopes by closely sorting out the richest particles of metal from larger masses of low-grade ores, and by waiting for the advent of railroads—balloon travel or what not—to bring the low-grade ores nearer and more cheaply to the means of reduction and realization.

These little camps of arrested development are the places to try men's souls. The hopeful heart that is cast away in one of these places must be a strong one, or the

wear and tear of existence, amid the weariness of
waiting, will break it more completely than ever did the
course of true love, running rough, crush out the pulse of
life's young dream.[1]

Despite the hardships of isolation, Mat found a place
for herself in the small community. For the first time in
her pioneering experience, she was completely familiar
with the travail of others, and life took on a larger
dimension. The other women in camp called on her for
help and confided in her. In addition, some of their male
neighbors—Rocky, Dillmer, McDonald, Crockett, and
Tipton—were in and out of the house frequently.

Mat was tolerant of Rocky, who was noted for his
sprees and his numerous lawsuits, which Mat followed
with some wonderment. For example, he stirred up
trouble when he unjustly accused Dick Anderson of
feloniously entering his cabin. Anderson retaliated by
suing Rocky. The case was put on Dr. Gally's docket,
dragged on for a number of months, and finally was
decided in Rocky's favor. Of the early comers who were
close to the Gallys, Rocky was the first to give up and
leave the country. In the latter part of April, he settled his
affairs and before leaving, dropped in to see Mat. "Mr.
Rocky," she noted, "came this morning to say 'good
bye'—is about leaving this section of country, & poor
man is entirely without means, having met with no
success in the sale of his mines."[2] He survived his reverses
and turned up again in a few months none the worse but
no wiser for his experiences.

Another neighbor, Mr. Dillmer from Alabama, had
been one of the founders of the camp and suffered ups and
downs with the Gallys. His cabin and plot of land were
close to theirs. Mat welcomed the opportunity to chat with

him, kept track of his activities and trips, and performed little neighborly acts for him. Their friendship, however, did not preclude bickering and quarreling between Dillmer and the Gallys. These quarrels usually revolved around the Gallys' hogs and Dillmer's garden. The hogs threatened his crop of pumpkins, cabbages, radishes, corn, and melons, but the animals were not easily deterred. Dillmer asked the Gally children to move the hogs to some other location, a request which made Mat exclaim: "More fuss about the hogs. Mr. Dillmer entertains the most absurd notions about the matter—says if he was to plant potatoes by the roadside & they (the hogs) ate them we (or their owners) would be responsible."[3]

The doctor did drive the hogs to the valley, an act which took much time and effort, but there was no keeping the animals away from the canyon. Later, Mat waded through the high grass "until I was wet to my knees"[4] in an attempt to head the pigs away from the gardens. Tiring of the commotion over the hogs, Mr. Dillmer finally gave in and built an enclosure around his plot. Mat, however, continued to be suspicious of him. "The spotted sow," she complained, "is dead owing I suppose to the injuries rec'd from Mr. Dillmer."[5] She recorded his transgressions, denouncing him for claiming possession of the water in the lower part of the canyon and seeking to buy Fergerson's garden for $60 in depreciated notes. For all her suspicions, however, Mat permitted him to confide in her. Fate was not to be kind to Dillmer, and like several other Hot Creek neighbors, he would pass out of their lives a year later and would be missed deeply.

Mat's relationship with Bob McDonald was smoother than that with Dillmer. McDonald came in often to sit and chat and participate in the family's activities. One evening in January, for example, they amused themselves by tracing on a wall map the routes to the southern California counties. After this exercise, the doctor spoke at some length about the habits and manners of the regional Indian tribes, information he had picked up while talking to former Indian agent Colonel David Buel.[6] On an evening visit in February, the doctor went off to bed leaving McDonald with Mat. She was peeved and declared that "the Dr very impolitely went to sleep and I was not very entertaining. Miss Gregory here for a recipe. Life monotonous."[7]

Dr. Gally's closest Hot Creek friend during the first half of 1868 was Tipton, but the friendship which began so warmly deteriorated when Tipton and the doctor became involved in a joint business arrangement. The doctor had the habit of turning friendships into business ventures and always discovered that these partnerships were unsatisfactory in the long run. The Roberts Creek ranch enterprise had floundered because of disagreement with Tom; and an Austin partner, Bell, also had faded from Dr. Gally's life.

Tipton and the doctor had two major interests in common—prospecting and politics. They found a number of ledges, had the usual assays run, and experienced the same feelings of elation and depression while awaiting the results. Politics filled their leisure time; and Tipton, Dillmer, and the doctor organized the Hot Creek Democratic Club. Not all of the meetings were harmonious, however, and Tipton and the doctor provided most of the fireworks. The *Reporter* commented that when the doctor addressed the meeting, he was able "to touch the popular chord and he is always listened to with pleasure."[8]

Prospecting and politics brought Tipton directly into the family life of the Gallys. He helped out around the place, assisted Mat in the garden, and repaired equipment. His thoughtfulness extended to the children in gifts such as the loan of his pony and a lovely white rabbit skin for Matty and a boat whittled for James. In return for these kindnesses, Mat invited him to dinner and read the newspaper to him. The high point of the friendship between Dr. Gally and Tipton came in April, when the doctor's constable quit the job and Tipton was appointed acting constable.

During the summer months, however, the joint arrangement to work the ranch land led to trouble, and the doctor and Tipton quarreled. By August, Mat felt a definite dislike for Tipton. His habit of borrowing things on the slightest pretext irritated her, and she dubbed him "his Lordship." He came to borrow a pony to ride to the ranch and "then he told James that unless he had a mind to picket her & keep her all night for him he could let her go. Clever gentleman not only lend him the horse but feed & look after her!"[9] She became further contemptuous of Tipton when she learned he had gathered potatoes from Mrs. Fergerson's garden, which previously had been part of a larger property worked jointly by the Fergersons and Dillmer. When Tipton balked in settling his account with the doctor, Mat was furious:

> He got $100 from Mr. Leon to see about or to spend in the Faigler precinct & thinks himself a millionaire. When the Dr asked him this morning for the $8 he charged for the hauling, the old rascal plumply refused to pay, also refused to account for $18 recd by him at sales when acting as constable, or to pay $14.50 he owed the Dr as well as 12 or 15 dollars on another account. He is an outrageous old scamp.[10]

In November, Hot Creek saw the last of the "consummate old rascal." He rode out of camp for White Pine on a horse borrowed from Dillmer, carrying one man's vest and another man's coat.

Family life suffered as the camp declined. A number of families were unable to withstand the extreme hardships and difficulties and broke up. Of the seven family women mentioned in Mat's diary, four separated from their husbands. With some money in hand, the produce of their gardens, and common living arrangements, two of the women were able to survive until their husbands returned to the family fold.

The most frequent callers at the Gally home were Mrs. Fergerson and her children. They often made long visits which broke up the monotonous loneliness of the days. Mrs. Fergerson held a tight rein on her little girl, Libbie, when they were visiting; but Libbie sometimes came over to the Gally place without her mother, and Mat did not care for the child. On one of her visits, Mat opined: "No one here excepting Libbie Fergerson who annoys me greatly."[11]

Nor did Mat's friendship with Mrs. Fergerson always run smoothly. One blowup occurred after Mr. Fergerson left for Pahranagat in mid-April. Mrs. Fergerson, in an advanced stage of pregnancy, came to Mat complaining that the Gally children were mistreating Libbie. Mat did not have kind words for her: "She is a poor foolish woman & now that her husband is gone will be sure to get into trouble—the Dr told her very quietly but decidedly that she must keep Libbie at home."[12] In the months to come, however, Mat and Mrs. Fergerson were drawn closer together by their loneliness and their common problems.

A most welcome visitor for Mat was Miss Gregory, who ran the Hot Creek boardinghouse. Mat's relationship with her was a warm one, and Miss Gregory was always ready to help her out in emergencies. Miss Gregory came to talk about recipes and to consult with Mat about her feet, which had broken out in eruptions. In early March, when she was seriously ill at the boardinghouse, Mat went up to look after her for a day or two until she began to mend.

During the second year at Hot Creek, Mat drew closer to the other women of the settlement. A few families resided in the upper settlement, and Mat occasionally saw Mrs. Wiggins, Mrs. Smythe, and Mrs. Rossiter. "The Upper Towners," she noted, "are so very kind & hospitable that I cannot avoid feeling grateful to them & I so neglectful of their courtesy. Mrs Smythe & Mrs Wiggins loaned me books."[13] Mrs. Wiggins impressed her more than any of the others, and she characterized her as a "mighty smart clever kind Yankee woman and her house is as neat 'as a pin.' Mrs W. insisted on our bringing home with us a pound of her fresh butter, which was very nice."[14]

Three births occurred in the settlement during 1868. The Rossiters' baby girl, whom Mat saw about three-and-a-half months after she was born, was a lovely infant, "as white as a lily," who flourished under her mother's care. Late in August, Mat stayed the night with Mrs. Smythe while she gave birth to a baby boy. More dependent on Mat than any of the other women during their pregnancies was Mrs. Fergerson. As his wife neared the end of her pregnancy and was unable to look after household affairs, Mr. Fergerson disappeared. On the morning of July 21, Mrs. Fergerson sent Libbie for Mat, who along with Mrs.

Shafer, remained with her until she gave birth to a baby boy. Mat related the event:

> I went in found her in great pain. I went for Mrs. Shafer & we stayed with her all day. [In the] afternoon she gave birth to a fine boy & this evening both mother and son are in good condition. It was the first time I had witnessed much less assisted at the great mystery of birth & I believe I was so much relieved as the woman herself when it was over. Mrs. F. sent for her friend, Mrs. Smyth[e], who declined coming. Mrs. Shafer then went for a Mrs. Potter who also refused to come so we were all alone, but I was amazed at the ignorance and superstition prevailing.

Mat took care of the newborn baby for several days. "Helping Mrs F.," she wrote, "who is trying to do her washing—poor woman she has a sore time!" The father had meanwhile turned up and immediately vented his ill-humor on his wife. A week after childbirth, Mrs. Fergerson poured out the details of her husband's insensitivity to Mat; Mat could corroborate that "he disowns his child & all such stuff—much of this I heard myself." Fearing more abuse from her husband, Mrs. Fergerson elicited Mat's help in moving into another place. Mr. Fergerson did not take kindly to the move and, arriving home in the dark, "swore dreadfully because he was unable to get into his house."[15]

Mrs. Fergerson's need for Mat was now particularly urgent. She sought Mat's help for both trivial and important matters. The last full day that Mat gave to Mrs. Fergerson went as many others had:

> Pleasant day, but a tiresome one to me. Got all ready to wash but was sent for to Mrs. Fergerson's, washed her baby, bathed her breast, brought her baby

home at 9 A.M. & kept it until 1 P.M.—took it up to her
& came home to get the dinner, but presently was sent
for, found her crying, made a poultice, brought the baby
back, cooked dinner with him in my [blank] & fussed
with him until 4 P.M. when her breast broke & Mrs.
Shafer appeared.[16]

Mrs. Shafer was another of the women in camp who
was having trouble with her husband. The mother of a
baby, Mrs. Shafer came to Hot Creek from Hiko and was
in camp several days before her husband found her. The
Shafers were German, and Mr. Shafer was a tailor by
profession. Why he wandered to the frontier is not known;
once there, he drifted around, and one story had him
wanted for cattle rustling in Belmont. With her husband
on the move, Mrs. Shafer found a protector and friend in
the Hot Creek butcher, James D. Page, who lodged the
forlorn woman and her baby in the back room of his
cabin. They became companionable, and Mat saw them
together at Mrs. Fergerson's place: "Shortly Mrs. Shafer
came in & presently Mr. Page. I was a little astonished &
greatly displeased at the familiar insolence of his manner
& of her gracious reception. I am afraid she has already
come to grief."[17] The familiarity between the two came
to an end when the Shafer and Fergerson women set up
housekeeping in the old Gerow house, which was without
a stove or fireplace but had the warmth of floorboards and
the splendor of papered walls. In November, Shafer
reclaimed his wife, although she was no happier with him
than before.

Even some of the women who had no serious
marital difficulties were burdened with the wayward antics
of their spouses. Shortly after Mrs. Smythe's baby was
born, her husband, along with the Miller boy and Mr.

Reno, made a drunken spectacle of himself. Mat castigated him for his behavior, and in the diary entry for September 11 suggested he "ought to be ashamed of himself! a good wife & a new baby." To his credit, he mended his ways and in mid December the Smythes made a visit to the Gallys' cabin with the baby.

The women in Hot Creek, like the men, took their relationships casually; the strain of living allowed for little choice in these matters. Miss Gregory, whom Mat liked so well, for example, conducted herself loosely in the months before she left the camp for White Pine. In June, she became friendly with Mat's neighbor, Mr. Dillmer, and by September the two were intimate. She spent a great deal of time with Dillmer, and Mat felt that as a result, her friend was deteriorating in both personal appearance and morals. When Miss Gregory came to obtain a saddle to ride with two others to Morey, Mat commented that "she is rougher & more untidy than I ever saw her."[18] Mat's staid sensibilities were shocked by Miss Gregory's open liaison with Dillmer: "She is quite a gay young woman in her style of travelling—she supped slept & breakfasted at Mr D's cabin, I presume being totally independent of womankind & all conventionalities." Sensibilities aside, Mat somewhat admired this adventuress, who would have "to try her fortune—not having the least idea of what or how she is to do—a brave women I think."[19]

Despite the instability of many frontier families, Dr. Gally believed in the benefits that a well-knit family could bring to society. He believed that the original school for education in the "pride of honor" should be the home. "This place that we call home," Dr. Gally wrote, "is really the Republic—or, in other words, the nation."[20] Here the child should be trained to live in society and to learn the spirit of good citizenship and common obligation. Pride nurtured in the home and tempered in the cauldron of public opinion was for Gally the proper way to educate individuals in ethics for a modern age.[21]

* * *

The autumn days in September were mild, although one night the wind sounded ''wild premonitions of the near approach of 'melancholy days.''' The Indians, Mat wrote, were ''gathering for the fandango, or rather pine-nut dance.'' A few fall flowers brightened the Gallys' cabin, but the Upper Town store had closed, and Mat noted that ''Joslyn might almost as well be, so poor is his assortment.''[22]

The pettiness, boredom, and uncouthness of the Hot Creek camp became more unbearable to Mat the longer she stayed. Drunkenness reigned periodically. The old-time exuberance of Rocky, Hinkle, and Gerow, who were no longer permanent residents, found ample expression in the antics of Reno, Tipton, Ellis, Smythe, and the Miller boy. The women were untutored and tiresome. The Fergerson and Shafer women, who crowded her little room with their squalling babies and noisy children, were increasingly bothersome. Mrs. Fergerson's ineptness in domestic matters irked Mat; after spending an entire day teaching her how to make a pair of pants, without much real success and while the children created bedlam, Mat was tired and angry.

All kinds of petty impositions made her fret. She had labored long and hard in sewing a coat for Mr. Reno, who paid an insignificant sum for her labors, but she remained silent ''as I do not expect to accommodate him again in sewing for him. I let it go, but I know Mr Shafer was right when he said $10 a small price."[23] Mr. Shafer irritated her with his quibbling about the money he owed the doctor on his meat bill. "The greediness of the little man," she confided in the diary on December 25, "makes him forget the great desire he has to be thought and treated like a gentleman."

Not less galling was the impudence of Captain Rossiter, who borrowed the Gallys' wagon from Mat, falsely telling her that the doctor had given him permission to take it. When Dr. Gally arrived home, he sent James to ask for the immediate return of the wagon. Rossiter replied that it was his understanding that the doctor had lent it to him and that he intended to use it for a week. Quite exasperated, Mat exclaimed: "Grand old rascal he is."[24]

The doctor brought suit against Rossiter, and about nine days later, Ed, the younger Rossiter, brought the wagon back without the tailboard and with the felloes of the back wheels damaged. He made profuse apologies and said he hoped the suit would be dropped. To avoid more trouble about the wagon, Ed later proposed to pay a dollar a day in greenbacks for the time the wagon had been borrowed. When the doctor refused the offer, the elder Rossiter appeared, worked "himself into a terrible passion, abused the Dr., refused to pay & at last pd the 35 dollars in greenbacks & left an order for Crockett to put in a felloe. The Dr. kept his temper & was quiet & gentlemanly."[25] The next day the elder Rossiter left camp with a harness and a horse collar that did not belong to him, leaving behind bad feelings among those he had successfully paid in depreciated greenbacks. One of his victims, Mr. Rooker, swore he would publicize him "as a swindler."

Mat was not alone in experiencing the little meannesses of the camp. The shabby treatment in September of Mrs. Cummings, who was managing the mill's boardinghouse, stirred Mat's indignation. Mrs. Cummings nearly killed herself by taking an overdose of opiates after learning of the nasty slurs cast upon her reputation. Mat flatly refused to countenance slander and she walked up the canyon to help the woman:

> After cleaning the house I went up again to Mrs
> C's—found her more comfortable—bathed & changed her
> clothing, bed etc—her hair which is extremely long &
> quite thick was full of mustard & difficult & tedious to
> comb out—but I succeeded in combing & braiding it.[26]

Shortly afterwards, the same woman incurred the wrath of Dr. Walter, who was intemperate in language and possibly deed. Mat pitied her, noting "Miss G. told me that Dr. Walter had quarreled with & abused Mrs. Cummings & that she was up there all alone."[27]

Even the Gallys' old friend Rocky, who had succeeded in business in Belmont and who had sent Matty "a beautiful crimson merino frock—all very nice but to[o] expensive for Rocky to buy & too gay for Matty under the circumstances," was cheated on a business trip to the camp.[28] Reno, whom Mat did not like, waited until Rocky went on one of his sprees and then bought his horse; Rocky did, however, recover the purchase money in a card game. Rocky should have known better, Mat thought, and he "deserved it to be so base and foolish as to incapacitate himself so completely," for he knew the unscrupulous character of Reno and his friends.[29]

Nevertheless, Mat had always had a good feeling about Rocky. Once, his arrival in camp surprised her in one of her blue moods, and he ''came in so kind & bright that it was a pleasure to see him,'' and he was encouraging, too, about the days ahead.[30] Several times in the midst of the harsh realities a small sign of human worth restored her equilibrium. For example, although she refused a friendly offer by Old Mose to work on the woodpile, she was moved by his thoughtfulness. ''I was,'' she wrote on October 11, ''grateful & surprised by his courtesy—old French gallantry not quite worn out yet in the old gentleman.'' Rarely did a visitor from the world of culture come to Hot Creek, but toward the end of the year, ''quite an agreeable finished gentleman,'' Mr. Cordoza, lifted her spirits when he stopped to chat en route to White Pine.[31]

Mat was, of course, very aware of the developing minds of her children. From their old friend Bell came the loan of Burns's poetry, which James and Matty eagerly read. Mat continued to press Shakespeare upon them and commenced drilling them in the rudiments of grammar. Quite frustrating to her were discussions with James on the subject of mesmerism. The boy's interest had been aroused by a book he had read, and he pursued his mother with questions that she honestly could not answer. James's inquiring mind also led him to the mill, where the machinery fascinated him. Although the thirst of the Gallys for culture had little direct impact on the community, one of James's friends, Smith Nelson, came by to ask if Mat would teach him to read at the same time that she was instructing James. So sincere was the request that Mat began the first lesson immediately.

The Gally family exerted a stabilizing influence at Hot Creek, but the basic insecurity of mining camp life posed a constant threat to family peace and harmony.

Mining communities fostered a sense of rootlessness that encouraged personal and social irresponsibility.

10

Borrasca and Bonanza

THE HOT CREEK camp struggled hard to remain afloat during the second half of 1868. The strikes in Rattlesnake Canyon had brought in enough men to warrant a boardinghouse, which Miss Gregory ran for R. V. Craig.[1] The Gillett ledge inspired confidence, and an assay run on its rock in September yielded an average of $100 a ton. The new Montgomery and Miller mill was operating by the fall, and Gillett had felt sufficiently confident in the camp's future to build a small mill of his own.

These hopeful signs did not persist, however, for already the White Pine mining boom was drawing people and money away from the outside camps. Pessimism about the camp's chances for survival was fed by several other tribulations. Colonel Raymond, whose mines in Rattlesnake Canyon had sustained the hope of the district, was encumbered in August with a $2,400 debt, and he was forced to close down his operations. Even worse, the poverty of the mines—most of them were yielding $30 a ton in assays—had become the subject of a letter to New York promoters declaring that the ledges "are & always have been a 'bilk.'"[2]

The Gillett mine was all that remained of the splendid promise of Hot Creek Canyon, and even this mine did not escape scandal as a result of the exposure of a fraudulent pulp assay of its rock. Gillett was so strapped for money that he could not pay what he owed to Mrs. Pascoe, who was running his boardinghouse. On October 16, Mat recorded:

> Mrs. Pascoe is trying to collect some of the board money for her wages & in some way she got into a wretched quarrel with Mr. Gillett. Not one cent has she received for her summer's work. The camp is in wretched condition. No money, no work everyone getting away but a few who still rely or hope for the fulfillment of the Raymond Company.

The mills had almost ceased operations toward the end of November. The Old Dominion mill, which had not been completely restored, was dismantled, and the boilers were transported to the plant of the White Pine Mill Company in Hamilton.[3]

People disgusted with the camp and its mines were moving quickly out of Hot Creek and were making whatever arrangements they could to dispose of their property. The Wiggins family transported their house to White Pine. Smythe was trying to find someone to take his business, Ed Rossiter was anxious to leave for White Pine, and the Old Dominion Company owner, Miller, had left for San Francisco. The store in Upper Town closed in September, and Joslyn's had very little merchandise to sell. In December, the Old Dominion saloon was moved to White Pine. There was no longer a blacksmith in camp, and the arrival of an itinerant tradesman in Upper Town, who pulled teeth and took pictures, drew from Mat the terse declaration that he "will find I think slight encouragement."[4]

By December, Mat counted only ten people still residing at Hot Creek, in addition to a handful of miners in the neighboring canyons. On December 9, she recorded in her diary that "there is left only five men in lower town & about the same number in Upper Town. The camp, mines & all completely deserted. Mr Garrett told me that Ophir Canyon was in like condition."

The doctor was downcast and depressed. Every step he took in the once humming camp recalled his shattered dreams: "Ah me! Ah me! The labors of old Hercules are child's play to the wasted work of the mountain men, whose thwarted monuments are crumbling now a-down the aisles of solitude." Rudely awakened from the exuberant daydreams of successful mines, he had to take stock of what was happening and of what was left to him. First had come the initial reality of seeing friends and neighbors pack their belongings to move on, and then came the symbolic pantomime of departure:

> Away goes the little cavalcade with a man in front leading, then a donkey or mule heavily loaded and girthed-cinched ... grunting a chorus of misery in tune with his steady step; and a man ..., or perhaps two men, bringing up the rear and stimulating the freight department.

The few men who waved farewell to the departing residents did not have the heart or courage to leave. As long as some ore was being mined, they stayed. This sorry handful of inhabitants eked out a bare existence while hoping that a new strike would change things. It was a lesson in endurance, as Dr. Gally knew: "Wait! Wait! Wait! Until the word gets so heavy on the heart that its spelling changes to 'weight, weight'—for the waiting becomes weighty."[5]

The disintegration of the Hot Creek camp was complete by late autumn. The rage of the day was the White Pine country, which was located in mountainous terrain about eighty miles north of Hot Creek. The mining district was not a new one. The prospectors had scurried over the hills in 1865-66, but little had come of their efforts until the discovery of the Hidden Treasure and the Eberhardt mines in 1867-68.[6]

When Dr. Gally was in Austin in mid July on political business, he discovered that the White Pine excitement was preempting politics as a topic of conversation. Throughout the southeast, established business interests feared the sudden impact of the White Pine boom. All during the summer, the press in Austin and Belmont tried to dampen enthusiasm for the area. The *Silver Bend Reporter* printed a letter from a White Pine correspondent that snickered at the extraordinary excitement produced by thousands of dubious claims and insisted that the district was noteworthy primarily for its pockets of silver ore.[7] The *Reese River Reveille* parodied the White Pine thinking and ridiculed the creation of a school district, the election of a board of education, the selection of a school lot, and provision for the remuneration of a teacher before a single child was residing at White Pine. Further titillating its readers, the *Reveille* reported the existence of a debating club; a nondenominational religious sect dubbed "The Universal Brotherhood"; and a reading room stocked with patent office reports, Tupper's *Proverbial Philosophy*, the *Bible*,

The Boy's Own Book, Baxter's Saint's Rest, the *Book of a Thousand Songs*, and newspapers.

The gibing did not lessen the interest in the White Pine mines, and toward the end of 1868, there were between 1,800 and 2,100 inhabitants in the three White Pine settlements of Hamilton, Treasure City, and Shermantown. Those who took a dour view of developments, however, believed that the population consisted mainly of "rowdies, gamblers, bruisers, dogs, puppies, and other loafers of notoriety."[8]

White Pine had created so much stir that Dr. Gally was anxious to rush up there along with everyone else, although the reports emanating from the new camp were conflicting. Anyone who had been involved in a mining rush knew that the first comers literally held monopoly rights over ledges and lots. Reports from White Pine indicated that there were individuals with thirty to forty claims each; and town lots which had cost $25 were selling for $150 to $200, and in some instances for $600 to $1,200. The temptation to run off to White Pine to see what it had to offer was difficult to resist.[9]

The beautiful weather of early September reinforced Dr. Gally's mood of wanderlust. All he needed was an excuse, and that nearly came when the owners of the Milk Ranche asked him to convey 1,500 pounds of butter to White Pine. They were unwilling to pay more than three-and-one-half cents a pound, however, and the arrangement came to naught.

Dr. Gally was given an opportunity to travel when he discovered that three men needed transportation. The day's excitement had made him tired and tense, and during the night he "had a miserable attack of pain wind & nervousness, but towards morning got easy."[10] The next day, those who had wanted to be conveyed were not on hand or not ready. The doctor talked of shelving his plans, but before the day was over, he had changed his mind. In short order, he had saddled Punch, packed Kit, and was off. Mat didn't want to see him leave and she wrote:

> I did hate to have him go off alone, but he thought best, particularly as he had agreed with a Mr. Carroll (I believe) to locate him in whatever he found, for which benefit Mr. C. payed him $30 in provisions 100 pds flour bacon coffee sugar etc. Matty & I watched him out of sight & then came home to lay down & cry like a goose. "Men must work and women must wait."[11]

During Dr. Gally's absence, acquaintances were filling Mat's ears with glowing stories of the mines at White Pine. One rumor told of a laborer named Mormon Jack, who had worked in Dillmer's hayfields several weeks before and who had barely a cent to his name. The story told that he had mined $12,000 from one ledge. Prudent as Mat was, she was carried away by the tales:

> The mines at White Pine still look gay—& the money that has been really made there is 'astonishing Pip! astonishing'! A man they called Mormon Jack who cut hay 6 weeks ago for Mr. Dillmer & who was in rags & not a cent has *realized* $12,000, has several men at work on his ledge bought himself a gold watch & stove pipe hat and turned gentleman at large—this is only one of many similar successes.[12]

A report that the doctor had discovered a ledge of considerable value, however, prompted Mat to comment, "I guess not."[13] She was, of course, waiting expectantly for his return. On the evening of October 5, he arrived home with the news that he had found several ledges, the value of which was uncertain.

In November, the doctor hauled 872 pounds of his own potatoes to White Pine. There, he experienced the excitement and frustration of his first major mining rush. Despite the cold weather, men hurried about their business "enveloped to the eyes in woolen wrappings, piled fold on fold, until the form and outlines of humanity were lost, jostled and collided with each other in the frozen cloud."[14] In a letter to the *Enterprise*, Dr. Gally described the feverish excitement:

> I suppose that there has not been, at any time, or in any place so complete and perfect a conglomerate of all that is human, voluntarily assembled, on earth. Brigham Young has sorted all creation, and specimens of his collection may be found at White Pine. California is there in all her varieties; and the railroad has sent down the newly arrived gent from Central Park in New York city, and other fancy localities. I grieve to say that this population is not as strictly careful about the rights of property as the old Californians were. Tools cannot, with perfect security, be left lying about loose as they could in old times. "Everything goes at White Pine," is a gay proverb in the camp. "Yes!" said a Dane who had bought some boots and goods for himself and distant family, and hid them overnight under his bed, "Everything goes at White Pine! mine poots and try goots goes, too. Somebody he steal tem lasht night."[15]

Where there once had been silence in a "weird and wayless world of rugged hills and dusty wastes," there was now the incessant babble of adventurers more stern-willed and adamant than the followers of Peter the Hermit "when he went prospecting for a graveyard."[16]

By this time, Dr. Gally was no longer the friendless greenhorn of 1864, and he had numerous friends and acquaintances at White Pine. From Belmont were the lawyers E. C. Brearley and D. W. Perley, who were suffering severely from the miner's disease, "Chloride on the Brain." Perley boasted of staying up all night by a ledge he had stumbled upon, "d—d near freezing to death waiting for it to get light enough in order to write the location notice." All the Belmont boys were boasting of their locations and were spending money generously. Several people from the Hot Creek areas were there. Miss Gregory, Mat's old friend, lost her cabin in a fire in White Pine. The impecunious and troubled Mr. Fergerson had suddenly prospered and boasted of owning a string of horses. The Rattlesnake Canyon mine owner, Colonel Raymond, had shifted his operations from mining to land speculation and, in partnership with Judge Walsh, was disposing of town lots.[17]

There was something grand about the combined work of man and nature in White Pine. From the slopes of White Pine, Mokomoke, and Treasure Hill, the great ranges of mountains rose to the east and west. The three settlements of Hamilton, Treasure City, and Shermantown were bustling communities. Treasure City, which was 9,200 feet above sea level, had an estimated population of 6,000 and Shermantown was inhabited by several hundred. By the spring of 1869, there was talk of 12,000 people in the White Pine Mining District. Treasure Hill was initially the center of mining activity there, and old Nevadans were comparing it to the Comstock of the flush days. Hamilton emerged as the commercial center of the district, while Shermantown had two quartz mills, a smelting furnace, and a number of sawmills by the beginning of 1869. There was work for everyone at five dollars a day, innumerable business opportunities, and, of course, money. Dr. Gally believed that few people knew where all this mad excitement was to lead:

> It is my honest belief that not more than one man in ten has any notion of what he is doing, is *to do*, or *ought* to do, or what he came there for, unless to—take a drink. Everybody talks big about ''big things'' which he owns, or has seen, or heard of, or is going to see when the snow goes off. Everybody talks about thousands of dollars, town lots, chlorides, claim disputes, putting a head on somebody and—take a drink.[18]

But Dr. Gally, like everyone else, had entered into the mainstream of excitement. After weeks of looking for accommodations in the White Pine area—rents and town lots at Hamilton and Treasure City were exorbitantly high—the doctor rented a cabin in Shermantown. A few days after the first of the year, he returned to Hot Creek tired and ill. Mat nursed him, and in time he was up and around, making minor repairs on the wagon and cart.

As soon as he was strong enough, Dr. Gally began packing up their belongings, but Mat did not share his enthusiasm. The people passing through Hot Creek deepened her gloom. One man had lost his provisions on the road, and since there was ''absolutely nothing in the town to buy,'' borrowed some bread from Mat.[19] A poor Irishman came along without a penny to pay his way, and Mat invited him to eat supper with them. On the first day of the new year, Mat was overwhelmed with a dark premonition: ''I am so tired tonight that I can only vaguely wonder what the New Year has in store for us. God help us to do our duty.''

The journey to White Pine and the first months of life there required patience and faith. Mat made no entries in her diary for three months, and not until April 15 did she discuss the high points of the trip, which began when they left Hot Creek for White Pine in mid-January.

> We drove slowly and got within three or four miles of Sherman early on the 22d—here we camped because the Dr heard that the house he had rented was not vacated as agreed upon. There was an inch or two of snow on the ground but we scraped away the snow put up the tent and after supper went comfortably to sleep. The Dr found on riding up to town there was some trouble about the house & consequently resolved to build one, although green miserable lumber is $300 per 1000 ft. With many discouragements he got the house up and the first week in February we moved in. The house was of course unfinished and indeed is still so.... About the middle of March the children were both attacked with typhoid pneumonia—the Dr prescribed for them and we nursed them ourselves. I scarcely slept at all for two weeks—they were both of them very sick but Matty was dangerously ill, and is just now able to go about. Her father treated her disease with great judgment and we think she will entirely recover without any ugly relapses.

Once located in Shermantown, the Gallys were caught up in the maelstrom. The White Pine mining towns were rougher and coarser than any they had previously known in Nevada. At White Pine, they plumbed the darker depths of human existence.

11

The Shermantown Episode

AT THE peak of the boom in 1869, there were between 10,000 and 15,000 people at White Pine. They were not provided, however, with effective government or adequate services, for without the benefit of meaningful county organization, vital tax-supported services could not exist.[1] Everything depended on private beneficence and individual energy. Civic-minded citizens in Treasure City and Hamilton raised $1,000 in April as an initial outlay for a hospital, and a Hamilton doctor offered a "pest home" to isolate smallpox cases. An enterprising individual opened a bathhouse in the spring.[2]

When the state legislature finally created a new county in April, much damage had already been done, for municipal organization had not filled the vacuum created by the absence of county government. For example, Shermantown was without a jail as late as the summer of 1869. The emergence of county government, however, did not mark the end of chaotic political and social conditions at White Pine. All too often, the needs of the community were compromised until they could no longer be overlooked. The county jail and hospital were totally inadequate. The unpaved, ungraded streets covered with slag needed improvement. Water, supplied from the pipes of a private company, was expensive, and wells were used wherever possible.[3]

The authorities inevitably made compromises that reinforced frontier liberty. The three White Pine communities were free and easy places where almost everything was allowed. Inebriated men slept out their drunkenness on the side streets of Hamilton. In the same town, show-offs rode bucking horses through the streets, jeopardizing the lives of pedestrians. Citizens made their own arrests in the absence of the police force.[4]

The lack of social responsiblity at White Pine caused those least able to look after themselves to suffer most. Unprotected women and dumb brutes were often at the mercy of the worst members of society. There were, of course, upright men at White Pine, whose generosities and charities revealed a high order of human goodness, but most people were too preoccupied in money-making schemes to think about the sufferings of others. The major impulse motivating community thinking was universally understood: '''Honor! Why how long have you been here? Honor's played out! People here are on the make! What d'ye 'spose they come here for?'''[5] A local resident observed that the dwellers in the Pogonip are ''swimming in a stream of incessant excitement, and must go on with the torrent, since they could not breast its wild waters and make head against the current if they would.''[6]

Each of the three White Pine towns was uniquely different. Hamilton, which became the county seat, owed its preeminent position to the labors of keen-witted California speculators, who had turned "inferior advantages to gold." Dr. Gally wrote a befitting description of the place:

> I have told you something about Hamilton. Hamilton is the county seat—a settin' in the snow. Two lines of heterogeneous houses flanking a river of mud. It is a very busy town, about half a mile in length by three hundred feet broad. It calculates to be broader when it gets its growth—in fact, the stakes are set so thick, to indicate town lots around Hamilton for half a mile, that the place looks as if intended for a Dutch vineyard. Hamilton is the place where we get what we live on, to-wit: whisky, bacon, and flour.[7]

The town displayed its raucous energies on Sundays as well as weekdays. In fact, there was more excitement on the Sabbath Day: idle men ambled the streets, auctioneers announced their wares, fruit peddlers noisily peddled their produce, and drunken men were everywhere.[8]

Treasure City, located in the clouds above Hamilton, had more people and experienced a greater degree of prosperity than did Hamilton. People in Hamilton jested that the altitude of Treasure City had intoxicated its inhabitants into believing that Treasure City was the heir to the civilization of Cuzco, Quito, and Potosi. Officials in Treasure City showed more rapacity than public spirit in assiduously enforcing local ordinances against unwary outsiders.[9] The citizenry made light of the bizarre specimens of humanity—"Buffalo Bill, Big Mouthed Jakey, Wall-Eyed Murphy and Horse-Head Brown, all of whom have recently arrived from California or Western Nevada"—who appeared on the streets. Crowds were given to stampedes, which were set off by almost any mishap: the collapse of a stovepipe or the prospect of gunplay brought out the saloon dwellers "like a flock of wild pigeons."[10]

Dr. Gally described the ludicrous sights offered by the city in the clouds:

> Treasure City street—there is but one—is crowded all day by a mass of male humanity, weaving in and out, tramping the slush snow underfoot, coughing up the fog, and taking a drink. . . . Blasts are set off in a crowd, somebody cries "look out!" and everybody looks up for falling rocks. Teams struggle through the street, over the stones, hauling wood, water, goods and lumber; teamsters curse; dogs fight in the snow-slush; men gamble heavily; houses are built on stilts, and we all—take a drink.[11]

The insignificant rival of Hamilton and Treasure City was Shermantown. Dr. Gally believed that it was better located, was more habitable, and enjoyed a warmer climate and a better supply of fuel than Hamilton. Unfortunately, Shermantown had not realized its potential. A few men had energetically built sawmills and laid down a road, while a great many others had laid off town lots for speculative purposes. The town, not more than a mile from the Eberhardt mine, had neither sufficiently good roads nor mills to capitalize on its location.[12] Shermantown, according to Dr. Gally, was a small-time affair:

> There is neither public spirit nor private munificence in Shermantown. The only real push I ever saw made to enlist the public of Sherman was the attempt made by Lew Moore, Sanford Hall and others to get up a benefit bumper for Miss Clara, the Bell Ringer woman. That was a noble joust! Splendid and magniff uprising of a generous and susceptible public! Gorgeous ovation of "Sleepy Hollow" in honor of female virtue! Yet

Shermantown is bound to be a town of importance, by virtue of natural advantages; and even now, in spite of narrow speculation, it grows steadily and somewhat rapidly. It is the most quiet town of the trio, but not altogether orderly—seems to be a chivalrous place, and has about one duel per month.[13]

Indecision in community affairs was coupled in Shermantown with high aspirations. The cost of supporting an incorporated town government was expensive—between $6,000 and $10,000 a year. A movement to disincorporate began under the leadership of Dr. Gally. The purpose of the agitation, which began even before Shermantown had a jail built, was to petition for a public vote on the question. The local newsheet called the idea hairbrained and was skeptical of plans to abolish the police force as long as the Sunday saturnalias made "Rome howl, terrifying the town with unearthly yells and reckless discharge of firearms in the street."[14]

Several civic improvement schemes were undertaken, however, and reflected some community spirit. The town fathers turned over a lot to the school trustees, and the lumber merchants contributed the wood for a schoolhouse. Two or three individuals attempted to launch subscription schools.

Other civic activities conveyed the idea of permanence. The Independent Order of Odd Fellows (IOOF) and the Masons jointly began work on a hall in June, and there were two newspapers in operation by the summer. The more cultivated citizens attended lectures delivered by Dr. Dehl on the "Asiatic East," the "Bible Lands," and "Egypt and the Pyramids." For patrons of the dramatic arts, a ballet dancer exhibited her talents, and an acting troupe celebrated the opening of the new theatre with a performance of the "Lady of Lyons." A circus and gymnastic show performed in a large tent, attracted those who could afford to pay the admission price, and the music emanating from the tent cheered those who could not. On the Fourth of July, celebrants were out in force, firing rockets and Roman candles, launching a large balloon, and speechifying. And on the anniversary of Maximilian's capitulation, the Mexicans celebrated with their own festivities.

Shermantown was insulated from the violence in and around the other White Pine communities, and news of particularly outrageous crimes shocked the "Sleepy Hollow" inhabitants. Mat was sickened by the report of a "dumb man killing & burning his friend" in the hills between Hamilton and Treasure City.[15] The closest Shermantown came to a riot was the tumult following a horse race that was held at the mouth of the canyon toward the end of July. "While we were at supper," declared Mat, "there was a great noise & crowd in the street—pistols drawn & much threatening but the police succeeded in dispersing the crowd peaceably—some commotion about the bets."[16] Marshal Bliss and Officer Smith acted quickly to disarm three of the troublemakers and averted serious trouble. The concern over the use of firearms within the city limits prompted the *White Pine Telegram* of June 18 to suggest the need for a city jail.

Dr. Gally had observed that few people knew why they were at White Pine or what they were to accomplish there. This was certainly his problem, too. He had staked claims to at least two ledges—the Black Point and the Great Sachem—in which he shared joint interests with several other men. The Black Point was the most promising of the two; and the doctor, his friend Adam

Hall, and James took out some rock in early July. The assays indicated, however, that the actual yield was less than the cost of milling. To pay expenses, a ton of ore had to mill $125 in silver bullion and the assay on their ore was only $70. In an article to the *Territorial Enterprise*, Dr. Gally suggested that the mines would produce at less cost with improved transportation:

> If tramways could be built from the top to the bottom of the mountain, and a short railway out to one of these big springs in the valley, near the base of the mountain, I apprehend that silver could be made with less labour and at less cost than by cutting tunnels for water and drawing ore with horses.
>
> This is a railroading era, and I think it is cheaper and vastly more pleasant in this barren country to feed a locomotive with white pinewood, and haul ore 10 to 15 miles to water, than it is to dig long tunnels for water, and feed horses on hay and barley to haul ore three or four miles. Wood is cheaper than horse-feed, and a railroad is as cheap as a long tunnel in loose rocks.[17]

A fever of impossible expectations was consuming men. All kinds of unlikely prospects seemed to contain an immediate promise of money. Dr. Gally spent considerable time prospecting with a companion in the neighboring ranges, but not much came of their efforts except exposure to the elements. In early July, on one of these jaunts, the doctor discovered a rich ledge during a hailstorm. He learned later that the ledge was a continuation of one already staked out. By August, there was hardly anything more left to discover and Mat, bemoaning the futility of their lives, declared: "Every day the Dr walks and climbs about the hills tiring himself out all to no purpose."[18] The Gallys had come to White Pine at the peak of the boom, in the early part of 1869, but by the middle of the year, the bonanza had ended. Most of the owners of claims refused to admit that they were worthless; the doctor refused to trade the Black Point for a ledge Mr. Hall had optimistically valued at $50,000.

While the bitter truth was being hammered home, Dr. Gally cast about for money-making opportunities. With the help of Adam Hall and James, he had built an icehouse and packed twenty tons of snow by the end of April. The icehouse was perfectly intact in June, but ice was selling at a mere three cents a pound. Even at that price, customers were difficult to find. Half the ice had melted by July and all hope of profit from the project melted, too. Dr. Gally briefly considered the stone quarry as a profitable venture. He abandoned this idea because although people were building stone warehouses, they either had their own supply of stone or were making purchases from one of several other vendors. For a while, he was optimistic about obtaining a contract for bricks; in desperation, he carried a bag of sand to Hamilton, hoping to wrench a contract from the builders of the new courthouse. Nothing came of this move nor of his attempt to sell his house lot as a valuable location for a millsite.

The closest Dr. Gally came to making a fortune at White Pine was as a result of the rock of two other men. The doctor had spread the word that two of his acquaintances had ore which was assaying $1,680 in silver and $100 in gold per ton. Judge Walsh became interested and said he could sell the rock in San Francisco. As the go-between, Dr. Gally obtained the rock for Judge Walsh, as well as 200 feet of the mine for himself as payment for his services. When a second assay was run, however, the yield was merely $20 per ton. With a load of worthless rock on his hands, Judge Walsh felt tricked; he sent Dr. Gally "to pay Dr. Robertson $100 if he would assay the rock in their presence & produce a result of even hundreds of dollars."[19] The assayer, Dr. Robertson, refused to be bribed and the matter ended there.

Nor was Dr. Gally fortunate in his two attempts to win appointment to public office. He was promised a seat on the school board and was endorsed by the county commissioners to become a justice of the peace. Someone else was appointed to the former post, and the attorney general had insufficient funds to cover the salary of a new justice of the peace. In regard to the former position, Mat wrote: "I expect the old gentleman's conscience reproached him so sorely for bestowing any office however good upon a Democrat that he cried out 'I yield I yield I can no more.'"[20] She summed up the disappointments by saying: "I am quite discouraged—we try so hard to get along & meet with no success—it seems there is no place for us in the world!"[21] Trying to overcome her sense of discouragement, she noted on May 21 that "I have been reading Bulwer's "Novel" awhile tonight—I often draw from it consolation."

With the exception of $64 earned in hauling coal to a charcoal oven, Dr. Gally had made no money at White Pine. He was typical of most White Pine residents who experienced bad luck there in 1869. The speculative fire had raged during 1868, but by 1869, the boom had collapsed. Rumors circulated that the Wells Fargo & Company, the California Bank, the Overland Telegraph & Express, and the San Francisco *Alta* had failed. Business had slowed and money had disappeared. Skilled workmen at the mills were asking and receiving $60 per month with board, but hundreds of others were taking any kind of work to pay for food. Many who had some money left were leaving the camp. Martha Gally summarized the situation succinctly in her diary entry of June 25:

> The truth is that the camp is so dull, so little money here, that there is no market, no demand for labor or anything else—men are working for $3.00 per day when ordinary wages have never been less than four dollars. Everyone is anxious and apprehensive. We cannot sell ledge, stone quarry, horse, lots, nor anything. I scarcely know which way to turn.

By the summer of 1869, the amount of bullion shipped out of the district had dropped, and it was becoming clear that a rich body of ore might not extend below the 100-foot level.[22] The ore deposits, moreover, were difficult to mine because they were cemented in limestone formations.[23] Reflecting this disenchantment, the cost of services had declined, and prices had fallen on town lots, wiping out large initial investments. At the same time, prices on many articles of merchandise were as high or higher than in 1868.

All during 1869, however, the district expanded unevenly. There was not much ready cash in the camp, but the mills were operating on a twenty-four-hour basis. Times were dull, but new mills were under construction, and piles of rock were waiting to be worked. Dr. Gally believed that the trouble lay in the fact that the boom had attracted more people than dollars. The fate of the district's future rested in the quantity and quality of its rock.[24] Everyone was awaiting an answer during 1869.

For the Gallys, the gamble at White Pine was a disaster. Mat found neither rewards nor satisfactions, and she was more of a martyr than ever, enduring people, poverty, and illness. She put up with the comings and goings of her husband's many friends and acquaintances.

Sometimes snappy in her private judgments, she characterized Adam Hall, the doctor's partner in the icehouse venture, as "very stupid," "very tiresome," "very tedious," and "kind of selfish." Hall was not altogether without redeeming qualities, however, for he volunteered to drive the Gallys' horses back to Hot Creek. Another "insufferable bore" and "awfully tedious" fellow, John W. Graves, interrupted Mat's household work and would sit for long stretches of time voicing his discontent with frontier life. "He is so dismal," she wrote, "as to be disagreeable—thinks he has lost all he has invested in the camp."[25] A casual visitor, Dr. Crowell, was dubbed a "fussy little fellow that I did not fancy—though he was excessively civil," and when he turned up later to berate her for not sending the children to the Sunday School, she labeled him the "abominable old Dr. Crowell," whom she would send packing the next time he came around.[26]

There were a few of the doctor's friends that Mat respected and enjoyed. Fent McDonald amused her with his belief in spiritual mediums. She had a kindly feeling toward Mr. Allen, who sold bottled cider, beer, and pop and who sent her refreshments and a book now and then. At first she declared "I should be obliged to him if I liked the cider or fancied Maryatt's novels,"[27] but because he was James's friend, she adopted a softer approach. James spent much time in Allen's shop and assisted him in various ways, and Allen showed his appreciation by taking James to the circus.

In addition to the doctor's friends, there were people from neighboring families who visited Mat frequently, and she was well acquainted with the mishaps of her neighbors. John Clarke, who had helped the Gallys build their Shermantown cabin, had become involved with a

Danish woman while her husband was away. When the master of the house returned, the unhappy wife sought Dr. Gally's advice and asked him to act as a go-between in the love triangle. The doctor, seeing her agitation, "had the necessary conversation with Mr. Clarke afterwards."[28] In a darker vein was the news that Dr. Gally's favorite friend, Mr. Martin, was killed in his own house, leaving behind "7 children the oldest a boy, blind, the next boy with his legs amputated at the knees, four girls and a baby boy—the murderer as usual escaped."[29]

A few women set examples for Mat in their strength of mind and will. The schoolteacher, Mrs. Shoaf, was the mainstay of her family during the prolonged illness of her husband. Another neighbor, Mrs. Addington, left in the lurch by her husband, had promptly turned to supporting herself as a seamstress in a local shop.

Although Mat had no binding ties to the other families in Shermantown, the Sweeny family was an exception. Mr. Sweeny brought his wife, a woman of twenty who possessed "a fine good face," and two small children to Shermantown in June. Shortly after their arrival, Mat visited them and concluded that Mrs. Sweeny was "not a woman of much culture but kind and good."[30] Since Mrs. Sweeny was pregnant at the time of her arrival, Mat began sewing a baby's gown for her. Unfortunately, the two did not get along well at first. Mrs. Sweeny's pregnancy and Mat's poverty evoked irritability. Mat sold Mrs. Sweeny a tablecloth and nightdress at half value, and Mrs. Sweeny then refused to pay her. Mat, exploding with resentment, declared Mrs. Sweeny was "a close selfish woman—last night I worked some buttonholes etc on a coat she was fixing. I did half the work for which I was paid $2 and yet because she knows I need the money is willing to buy things at the lowest possible price."[31] Mat found Mrs. Sweeny increasingly "tiresome," but after the birth of the baby in September, the two forgot their quarrel. Mat noted that she was "very agreeable & has a dear little baby. I really enjoyed holding him."[32]

The Whitall, English, and Olds families also visited the Gallys, but no real camaraderie emerged between them. Both Mrs. Whitall and Mrs. English rubbed Mat the wrong way and she complained "they are very disagreeable to me."[33] Matty was friendly with the daughters in these families, although her friendship with the Blaser and Olds girls did not begin auspiciously. The Blaser girl asked Matty to play with a black boy and girl, which she refused to do.

Mat continued to struggle with her usual concerns and tasks. She worried about her chickens, whose eggs were mysteriously disappearing, and she frequently discovered the chickens to be dead or missing. The dry weather in June and July meant that she and Matty had to tramp long distances over hilly terrain to find water. When the doctor was around, he helped carry the water and wring out the wash, which was Mat's heaviest job.

Although most of the days seemed wearisome and full of heartache, there were occasional lighter moments. The cats and a strange man in the privy provided one eventful day:

> Mrs. Nillson's old tom-cat got into the house with our cat & between the two I was awake much in the night. Some strange man in our privy. James told him it was a private house—he replied it did not look like it—which was true but he knew that he had no business there. However he did not go out very soon.[34]

Reading provided the greatest enjoyment for the

Gallys. During their stay at White Pine, Mat read aloud *Othello*, which precipitated a lively discussion about the character of Iago; *Coriolanus*, which elicited the remark that the hero "had no more faith in democracy than I have"; *The Pickwick Papers*, featuring the incomparable Sam Weller; *The Old Curiosity Shop*, which was completed "with eyes full of tears"; and *Cymbeline*, *David Copperfield*, and *Nicholas Nickleby*.

* * *

In the several months that the Gallys resided at Shermantown, the weather was rarely tolerable. The snow and the sub-zero temperatures of the winter months made frostbite common.[35] The snowstorms were so bad in April and May that visibility was limited to a few feet, and flakes of snow blew into the Gallys' cabin through the cracks. A late May storm brought drifts of snow seven feet high. The cold, bleak days prompted Mat to write: "Horrible weather—impossible I think in any other country. Snow and hail with terrific gusts of wind—roofs have been torn off and one large new canvas house blown down."[36]

The shift from winter to summer was sudden. After the wet snows and the cold rains of late spring, the days suddenly turned warm. By the end of June, the mercury was already registering in the high 90s. The hottest day of the summer came on July 23, when the mercury in the sun stood at 108 degrees before breakfast. August proved more bearable with heavy rains and showers, but September brought whirlwinds and blowing sand and gravel that blinded pedestrians. There was no escaping the wind, but there were those who found some solace in the gusts, as a Pogonip newspaper described:

> Men were compelled to keep their pants inside of their boots to prevent them (the pants) from being blown away: and as for the ladies, who had the temerity to venture upon the streets; many were to be seen in mortifying positions, revealing the meanwhile romantic scenes, which our extreme modesty forbade us enjoying.[37]

Inclement weather, polluted water, and poor nourishment combined to undermine everyone's health and to provide an environment in which common contagious diseases thrived. Whooping cough, dysentery, and diarrhea reached epidemic proportions in 1869. Children were particularly subject to whooping cough, and the death rate among the infants climbed. Mat recorded the death of three babies and one boy during August and September. She noted sadly that "Mrs. Harmon's little baby died last night—ah! poor mother!"[38]

The Gallys could consider themselves fortunate. The doctor was in good health except for occasional bouts with the hives, a sore throat, or indigestion. Mat became fearful when he remained in bed for more than one day. She wrote on July 5 that the doctor "had an attack of colic or indigestion, dyspepsia or something else which kept us up until 3 o'clock this morning—he suffers much—is oppressed, almost suffocates, his pulse is slow & his nervous system excited." She gave him large quantities of whisky, putting him to sleep. Her terrible premonitions "had her almost worried out," but the doctor felt much improved when he awoke.

The children, too, came down with common illnesses. Both James and Matty suffered from sore throats, neuralgic pains, and colds at times. The children looked pale and thin, and Mat blamed their poor health on the difficult climate and the high altitude. James was less able than his sister to withstand strain and deprivation:

> James up first; he was too tired to sleep; his father works him too hard. The Dr never had any judgment or mercy on children. When he works himself he wants everyone else to do as much. This morning we had nothing for breakfast but bread and tea so the Dr sent James (he would not go himself) to buy some meat on credit, which he succeeded in doing. James then went to Mr. Clarke's to get some coffee and sugar in the same way, but Mr C. refused. This was the first time the Dr was told that his credit was not good, and he was mortified. James hated to go to work; his poor thin arms are swollen.[39]

When the entire family suffered from upset stomachs in mid-August, Mat blamed the illness first on the heat and flies and not on the water. But this marked the beginning of serious bouts with diarrhea and dysentery for Mat and the children. Mat was unwell; large doses of whisky and laudanum eased the pain, but did not cure her condition. She was forced to remain in bed, complaining bitterly that "I am in bed because the Dr holds it the cheapest way to get well."[40] The children pitched in, doing the housework and preparing the little food there was in the house to eat. Mat was desperately in need of medicine for both James and herself, so the doctor, who was penniless, exchanged a small bar of crude silver for acetate of lead and opium pills, a tube for the syringe, and one dollar in change.

By the end of August, Mat had established her illness as dysentery. She suffered excruciating pain, and drugged herself heavily with opium. As her condition worsened, she resorted to alum, starch, and Dover's powders, but all with little real benefit. On August 31 she wrote:

Nearly two weeks today since I have been well. James
too is in bed feverish and restless. Matty not well either!
I am such a goose that I cannot bear the Dr to be away!
Poor fellow, sickness & not a cent! Was ever man so
worried!

Matters had become so bad in September that Mat
was bedridden and practically useless. Dr. Gally saw that
her condition was extremely serious and took a hand in
treating her. "The Dr.," she wrote, "gave me a dose of raw
flour & water stirred thick & black with pepper. It made
me very sick but I kept it down until I tried the second
dose which was too much. I was very sick all the
afternoon."[41] Her diary entry for September 10 illustrates
the critical state of affairs and the dilemma of a frontier
family trapped by circumstances beyond its control:

The Dr keeps a wonderfully good heart—we were never
so poor in our lives—we are almost in rags. He has only
4 old shirts that will not stand another washing and my
two calicoes I have worn constantly since I came to
White Pine & notwithstanding my turning & mending are
worn into rags. Matty is almost barefoot. We have had
no relish of any kind for weeks—nothing but bread,
meat, tea & most of the time sugar. And for me to get
sick at such a time! but the Dr is hopeful & patient;
better than I am. I write all this so if ever we see better
days we may look back at this experience & find that
man's endurance is wonderful. Our last 50 pds of flour
lasted us three weeks. I am sorry we were obliged to sell
our chickens! Vegetables are very cheap; corn 25 cts per
doz, potatoes from 3 to 5 cts, plenty of nice beets,
turnips, carrots, cabbage etc. James mended his boot. I
wish I was well. The Dr came home in good time
having been at Swansea to see if he could get a contract
to dig for water—but could not succeed. Two men killed
near Hamilton.

Mat's physical suffering was aggravated by frequent emotional upsets. The sight of a disheveled and bruised Matty, who had fallen while running from a dog, shocked her. When James came home violently ill, Mat immediately rose from her own sickbed. The boy looked and acted strangely—"faint, cold & hysterical; sobbing and chocking, the veins in his forehead swollen much, the skin red and his eyes bloodshot."[42] Mother and daughter rubbed his limbs, covered him warmly, and gave him brandy, and before long he was himself again.

Mat survived her illness only to be confronted with the absolute penury of her family. The doctor had made no money from his mines, his icehouse, or his stone quarry, but he was always on the verge of making a fortune:

> The Dr. at home not an hour all day; he is hot on a new speculation that is to take up some of the hay land that is unjustly (as he thinks) claimed at Duckwater—he is very anxious & excited about it, but I am sure it will end in nothing.[43]

Without the occasional money earned by eleven-year-old James, the family would have suffered even more. He worked at odd jobs; sold bottles, cider, and squash; packed bags with sawdust; and hawked eggs and chickens for his mother. He sold his mother's best table linen for several dollars, but he had no luck selling newspapers on commission. Mat observed that "he tried his papers again today, but made only 25¢ & walked so far too."[44] A nonpaying job such as decorating the ballroom with flowers was a pleasure, but the poverty of his parents forced him to help make ends meet.

At White Pine, the Gallys faced their worst crisis as a family. The question in mid-summer was how they were to survive. There was no money in the house and no prospect of obtaining any from the sale of their properties. They were not able to replenish their supply of candles and had to retire for the night at dusk. Mat could not even replace a lost comb "in the collapsed state of our finances." They were living on extremely short rations, making do with bread and tea. "We cooked," she declared on July 18, "the chicken for breakfast & ate bread & tea for supper. I don't know what we shall do!"

On the following day she was dunned for a $63.90 bill which she could not pay. James saved the day by selling the chickens for $25, and for the first time in several days they had a breakfast of beefsteak. Mat made needed purchases of candles, bacon, molasses, a bag of flour, and shoes for Matty, but in ten days she had merely $3 remaining.

Mat bewailed not having gone on to California in 1864. She had heard from Mrs. Sweeny that her father had purchased a farm in California for $300 in 1861; it was worth $3,000 in 1869. "What a mistake," she cried, "that we ever stopped in this miserable country!"[45] "Sometimes," she wrote a number of weeks later, "I reproach myself bitterly that I ever feel to complain of my lot—after all my shoulders might be sorer with another burden. God grant us truth & patience."[46]

The doctor was as desperate as Mat. He had counted on receiving $200 from Mr. Rocky for ledges deeded to him, but everything hinged on Rocky's sale of the ledges to J. D. Emersley. This hope was dashed a month later. Business conditions were so desperate that there was no possibility of employment. "There is," Mat wrote on August 2, "nothing doing & one cannot give property away. Many persons are going away, indeed everyone who can do so." The doctor drifted aimlessly, walking miles over the hills each day and accomplishing nothing. His boots were worn down and he had to tack on a sole before he could answer a court summons.

The doctor vented his feelings in a short poem written on July 18 at the peak of the ordeal:

> I said to the team which steadily strode
> To the jangling bells and the heavy load
> > "Get up!"
> For I was a driver of horse and of mule
> Taught, what I knew in Adversity's school
> Taught to "stick and to hang" on the hill
> To pull then together and shout with a will
> > "Get up!"
>
> Jingling! jangling! Steady and true
> Do like a mule what a mule should do—
> > "Get up!"
> Though there is ice and they slip and fall
> Hold them together—its bad if they sprawl—
> None overdoing and none overdone
> Steadily pull them as if they were one
> > "Get up!"
>
> I said to myself as I dustily rode
> In the hot summer sun on the alkali road
> > "Get up!"
> What if I am but a driver of mules
> Brains can be sharpened as men sharpen tools
> Stick to it—hang to it—pull with a will
> Life is a load—and we travel uphill
> > "Get up!"
>
> End it in weal—or end it in woe
> Do like a man what a man should do
> > "Get up!"
> Though there be blunders and often you fall

> Get up and pull again! never say "stall";
> It's no use to growl, and say "it don't pay to"
> Where there's a will there must be a way to
>   "Get up!"

The price they were paying for remaining at White Pine made less sense with every passing day. Mat had spent the last dollars on a can of jam, (for which she paid seventy-five cents), four-and-a-half pounds of potatoes, small white beans, onions, and beefsteak. The doctor managed to make $64 selling and hauling charcoal, $30 of which went to pay bills for the shoeing and keeping of the horses. They were at least "glad to have something to eat,"[47] but there were still several bills to pay. Mat calculated that $150 would pay an Austin bill for $124.38 and other small balances at White Pine, but where could the family obtain the money? The smelting works, which had bought the charcoal, was having trouble with its machinery and temporarily needed no more fuel. Toward the end of September, the Gallys were without money again.[48]

By September, the doctor was wondering how he could extricate himself from the White Pine disaster. All aspects of the district were disintegrating. Robberies and violence were common. "There is so much desperation & violence," Mat wrote on August 12, "that very few men carry money about them." One man, who was deeply in debt, committed suicide with a dose of strychnine. Wherever people turned there was talk of sickness, death and violence. On August 22, Mat recorded:

> There is a great deal of sickness in the camp, dysentery, diarrhea, whooping cough etc; also much suffering from insufficient means. A miner, who lived in a cabin down the canyon has been staying for a week or two at Mt

Ophir; yesterday he returned & after going into his house found lying upon his bed a dead man; upon examination the body was found to be in a state of partial decomposition. Some poor fellow with no home, no friends, no bed, no money crawled in & died alone. Last night a man was robbed about dusk of $38 between this place & Treasure City. God give us patience.

In the midst of personal and community troubles, however, Dr. Gally did not lose his nerve. To save expenses, he ran the horses over to the Duckwater valley in mid-August where they could forage for their own feed, and he walked the long distance home without complaining. To maintain his spirits, he wrote many letters and poems for the newspapers. Had it not been for the hard times, Putnam and Goodwin of the *Inland Empire* would have hired him.

By September, a decision had to be made whether to leave or stay. Mat was still suffering from dysentery. Matty was running around in tattered clothing and wearing torn shoes. "Matty," cried Mat on September 6, "needs new shoes & is growing old enough to feel sensitive regarding her appearance." James was sick, too, and he appeared run-down. "What will become of us I wonder. It makes me sick to think," she wrote on September 8, "but the Dr keeps a good heart." On September 9, Mat had only the fifty cents that James had earned filling bags with sand. Matters were so critical that Mat poured out her worries: "If I were only well & we had something to do." She spent her last quarter on September 11.

The Gallys' hopes for White Pine had come to naught. Mat recalled that a year ago, the doctor had "started on a long prospecting tour alone: I cried then and felt as badly as I do now—worse." The doctor had to borrow eleven dollars to pay for needed purchases—a bag of flour, $4.50; yeast powder, 37½ cents; meat, 75 cents; whisky, 50 cents; candles, 50 cents; butter, 75 cents; and potatoes, 50 cents. Mat had 50 cents left on September 14.

Circumstances improved when the doctor was offered a job hauling freight to Hot Creek, for which he received $20 in advance. On September 19, he rode over to Hot Creek to get his horses. For Dr. Gally, the trip to Hot Creek freed him of his cares. Autumn mildness was in the air, the ranchers were working the hay and hunting ducks near the springs, and there were signs of mining activity at Morey. The Shoshones had completed harvesting the pine nuts and were celebrating:

> I met a long train of my native friends and acquaintances on foot and on ponies, dressed "some in rags, and some in jags," but none in "velvet gowns." The most eminent members of the tribe invited, and in fact insisted upon me going to the dance, towards which they were winding their way. They said there would be heaps of "tee-kop," heap "a yan-a-kee" (laugh), and a heap of something else which I will not now mention.[49]

Promptly upon returning to White Pine, the doctor ordered the family to begin packing for a return to Hot Creek. They were not leaving any too soon, for already the water in the pails was freezing at night and clouds of dust whirled through the air during the day. What lay ahead could be no worse than what they were leaving behind.

12

Ebb and Flow

For MAT, leaving White Pine was a great relief. On October 1, 1869, they said goodbye to their neighbors, the Whitalls, turned the cabin over to Sanford Hall to cover his investment in the property, and as the mills sounded their whistles at one o'clock, they started down the canyon in their wagon. Two men, Galloway and Winnen, accompanied them. The first night out, Mat "laid in the wagon & listened to a long confab upon the proper culture of cabbage among some ranchers."[1]

The travelers spent a week on the road, and both Mat's strength and her appetite returned. She felt free of the harsh realities of the White Pine mining camp. Everyone they met on the road was kind to Mat. One rancher, who lived near the road, rode over with a gift of milk and potatoes, and hospitably offered them the run of his ranch. Another rancher gave Matty a three-month-old colt which had belonged to his little boy:

this little boy died about a week ago & during his illness
the colt had been neglected so much that he was scarcely
able to stand up. He is improving now, but I can't see
how we can get him to Hot Creek or what to do with him
when there, but Matty is delighted & has made him a
halter.[2]

Mr. Galloway, one of their traveling companions,
was "just as agreeable as one could desire,"[3] but Mr.
Winnen became sick the second day out on the road. Mat
had taken a liking to Winnen, whose entertaining account
of his native Cornwall had captivated her. At first it
appeared he had a simple cold, but he worsened gradually
and acted "so queer that I can make nothing of him."[4]
The man was wretchedly sick for weeks at Hot Creek, and
Dr. Gally diagnosed his condition as pneumonia. Dr.
Riddle, who came over to see him, diagnosed his illness
as typhoid fever.

At Hot Creek, the Gallys picked up the pieces of
their shattered aspirations, although nothing was as they
had left it. The dilapidated condition of their cabin
mirrored the decay of the camp. Mat's impressions of the
homecoming on October 8 were indeed mixed ones:

We got into camp about 5 o'clock P.M. & miserably as I
felt; my heart was glad. The house looked dismantled &
desolate, but they were all so glad to see us & so kind that
it seemed like getting home. Mr. Joslyn invited us all to
supper & Mrs. Foster, his housekeeper was very pleasant,
but I was too tired to eat. Mr. Crockett & Mr. Wehalie
helped us unload, Mr. C. brought us some wood & we
soon had a roaring fire though the night was warm. Mr.
Galloway brought me a bottle of wine, which though not
of good quality tastes pleasantly.

Many of their old neighbors had moved on or were
dead. Dillmer, who had squabbled with them over the

hogs, had died of smallpox. Both Mr. and Mrs. Wiggins, the neighbors who had resided in Upper Town, had succumbed to smallpox a few months after coming to White Pine. Another Hot Creek resident, Green Smith, had perished of the same disease. Wash Hinkle, the Hot Creek butcher, had died of pneumonia, which had been aggravated by excessive drinking. Danish Johnson had been killed in the Patterson district, and their old friend Rocky had nearly died after a reported attempt to castrate him. As for the old families, they had drifted off with the exception of the Smythes and the Randalls. Mrs. Fergerson had been reconciled with her husband, and they had gone to Pahranagat. Mrs. Shafer had taken up with Lafayette, Joslyn's cook, and they disappeared from the camp while Mr. Shafer was away from home.

As happy as Mat was to be back at Hot Creek, her old dysenteric problems returned. She suffered severe abdominal pains again and could do little around the house. On October 10, she wrote: "The house & children are deplorably dirty & I am lying on the floor. Hope & patience." Had it not been for the kindness of the neighbors, the children would not have been adequately fed. The doctor thought that some of Mat's trouble could be the result of the large amounts of lead she had ingested with opiates, but later he changed his mind and ascribed her condition to a malfunctioning liver. Her strength was slow in returning, and she felt drained of all energy.

Fortunately, Hot Creek was free of typhoid fever until the autumn of 1868. Typhoid bacilli, transported to Hot Creek by Mr. Winnen, who had managed to survive his illness, was contracted by the village blacksmith, Mr. Crockett. For several days before he became sick, he had been in and out of the Gallys' cabin. He had provided Mat with milk and vegetables, played ball with the children, and had begun to teach Matty how to milk his cow. Toward the last week of October he was feeling badly, and Mat prepared food for him and sent James over to his cabin to help out.

As Crockett's condition worsened, Dr. Riddle was called from Belmont. He diagnosed the trouble as typhoid pneumonia, and everything was done that could be. Mr. Williams gave him a mustard bath and rubbed him down with brandy. But Crockett sank into a coma, and Mat, who went to his cabin shortly before he died, reported that I "did what little could be done, but Mr. Williams is there constantly. Mr. C. did not know me at all—did not even rouse."[5] Crockett was buried on November 4, and Mat described her feelings about that somber event:

> A little after 4 o'clk P.M. the mares carried him to the grave, everybody in camp (almost) following; the Dr made a few brief but pertinent remarks & in the clear rosy glow of the sunset we came away & left Crockett quietly lying in our mother's bosom, the future no more mysterious than the past, & equally in the control & guidance of the great Father. Our children grieved deeply & sincerely. Crockett was their closest friend in camp & James had been much with him during his sickness.

The death of Crockett prompted the doctor to use him as a symbol of the men who lost their lives far from home and family:

> Crockett was smith to a miners' camp.
>   And some of us "boys" were there;
> He wasn't an angel—he wasn't a scamp—
>   But human as most of us are.
>
> "I thought," said he, "in a dream just now,
>   That I was away back home,

With apple and peach trees all in a blow,
    While fire flies danced in the gloam. . . .

"But, as I was saying, I thought it was me
    A-going along by the fence,
To the home that I left in '53—
    And never been back there since—

"For you see I came out, from Tennessee,
    To the coast, a good while ago,
And I've always intended once more to see
    The old place but you know—you know"—[6]

The few women who still lived at Hot Creek favored
Mat with many small kindnesses. Mrs. Foster, who was
running Joslyn's boardinghouse, brought food over
regularly and tried to provide moral support, but she had
her own problems with Joslyn, who withheld needed
supplies for the pantry. Mrs. Randall was helpful, and her
girls, Sarah and Alice, were frequent visitors before the
family moved from the lower settlement to Upper Town.

Mrs. Smythe, who resided with her family in Upper
Town, was pregnant and encountering complications of
her own. On November 11, fearing a possible miscarriage, she sent for Mat.

This morning while I was washing the breakfast dishes
Mr. Smyth came for me to go directly up there as his
wife was "flowing" to death. I went up directly & found
her with white lips & faint pulse & they surrounding her
with hot wet rags. I applied cold water plentifully, gave
her brandy & soon checked the hemorrage—stayed until
dark when I came home leaving Mrs. Randall with
her—she will probably have a miscarriage.

The baby was lost a few days later, and Mrs. Randall
brought down the fetus for Mat to view. As Mat was fond

of saying, there was "na'er luck" around the camp or the house.

The Hot Creek camp had not recovered from the collapse of 1868. There was the same optimistic talk about reopening the Old Dominion mill, and Emersley, who had leased the mill, had ordered the necessary boilers. But either because he lacked the funds or foresaw other difficulties, he dropped the matter. A small cause for celebration was the purchase of the Pure Metal mine by White Pine businessmen.[7]

Odd jobs were available, and the doctor was employed by Joslyn to make a freighting trip to Austin in early November. He began the journey in bad weather, complaining of chest pains and a skin irritation. During the trip, he injured his finger; it became infected, and when he arrived home, he was in considerable pain. Mat began immediately to treat the finger with "bread and milk" poultices, hoping the infected site would swell and discharge, but this did not occur. The doctor's temper grew short, and Mat complained that he was "as irritable as ever & more so."[8] For almost a month, he was preoccupied with his finger, and except for working around the cabin, he did nothing.

The doctor's infection made him increasingly short-tempered; he flew into rages without provocation. James did most of the work around the house, chopping the firewood and tackling other chores while his father grumbled. Mat blamed the doctor's irritability on the heavy doses of laudanum he had taken. Matters had become so bad by December that "the Dr sits constantly in the house and cannot endure the least noise, so we have a tedious time."[9] Even after his finger had mended, he was "so insultingly cross and abusive"[10] that Mat was glad to see him leave the house.

The doctor's illness had destroyed any chances of his earning some money, and once again, the family was running short of food. Mat earned nearly $20 selling bread to the Indians, who eagerly devoured it and came back for more, but she was disheartened by their reverses. On December 1, she bitterly observed:

> We cooked all of the bacon tonight; bread, potatoes & tea
> must suffice tomorrow. I took off my only chemise
> tonight to wash it & it is now hanging frozen on the line
> with my undershirt. I don't much miss it. The Dr. is even
> minus tobacco, which does not decrease his irritability.
> The papers told us of the death of Mrs Martin of
> Hamilton—her husband was murdered last summer & she
> now dead leaving seven children alone & unprovided for;
> the oldest a boy of fifteen with both legs off at the knees.
> I have no complaint & we will eat our bread and potatoes
> patiently & endure our sore fingers with what grace we
> may.

Thanksgiving Day was celebrated with only codfish balls for dinner. There was little to celebrate, but Mat still possessed an inner sense of fortitude. The absence of even the minimal necessities—candles, a pair of shoes for Matty, a table and other articles of furniture—made her very aware of their poverty, but she refused to admit that she felt poor: "Somehow I don't mind the bread & potatoes," she wrote on December 17, "& although we can turn nothing into money, I don't feel poor."

The old loves of her life afforded enormous pleasure. She and the children read Shakespeare, Plutarch, and Scott, and the days seemed less dull because she was occupied mentally. "For all we have so little money," she declared on December 25, "we are 'jolly' enough.

We have lots of fire some books & papers & a heap of talk. I began 'As You Like It' again. The children never tire of Shakespeare."

The doctor found relief from his nagging worries in working sporadically around the house. The back end of the cabin had collapsed and had to be repaired. Without being asked, he began building a stone storage room, roofed with timber, to adjoin the cabin on the east side. The doctor and James also made a needed chair, which Mat welcomed as "a source of comfort to all of us." A cold snap in mid-December had the doctor repairing the roof, tacking up a cloth ceiling, and erecting a partition with a door that made two rooms out of one. A few alterations in the fireplace provided more warmth.

After five years of floundering on the frontier, poverty had become a way of life for the Gallys. The primary goal was to get enough to eat, and as the old year ended, the monotonous fare of bread and potatoes was all Mat could put on the table. She complained that she was "so hungry for something besides bread & potatoes." By January 12, 1870, the situation once again appeared hopeless, and Mat felt despondent:

> The Dr accomplished a "plug" of tobacco & "bums" a drink of whiskey every day, so he is enabled to get along—& then he gets a square meal every day or two at some of the cabins; but we have no change—dry bread & praties; coffee with neither milk nor sugar. I felt quite sick, but when James came home with a nice beefsteak which we cooked, I got better. Felt like I had taken brandy.

Matters worsened, and on January 19, Mat noted:

> We did not cook potatoes for breakfast but ate toast with an onion, a little frozen, that the Dr picked in Joslyn's

garden. He (the Dr) is begging or stealing his tobacco
and whiskey—I am really ashamed of him. I see no
prospect ahead; the flour is most gone & we have only
$2.50.

Fortunately, the Gallys were not driven to begging, for
Joslyn extended credit for a bag of flour and other
necessities, which helped out until Mat could sell bread to
the Indians. Unable to afford soap, Mat washed the
clothes in lye water.

During these moments of desperation, the sight of the
doctor loafing around the house brought on a storm. "The
Dr.," lamented Mat on January 8, is "loafing & disputing
scripture, which is always unprofitable." When he
complained that he had no tobacco, she criticized him for
spending more money on that one article than he spent for
the clothing of the children and herself. Her open disgust
made the doctor sullen, but after his finger began to
mend, he tried hard to find remunerative work. A freight
job, offered by Emersley, came in the nick of time, for
Mat's patience had worn thin:

The Dr is cross & abusive; because there is only a little
bread (flour) he wants the children to eat—nothing but
potatoes, though he himself eats more than half of
everything in the house, always selecting the best. I think
bread (not plentiful) potatoes (in abundance) salt (not
always) meat (very occasionally & then James gets it) tea
& coffee without sugar or milk is poor food for children
to live on for months & then to be continually scolded is
too much. The Dr can always buy or beg whiskey &
tobacco, (though he has not been really down since
May/69) but the children must go hungry & ragged. I
don't mind my own want, though I have only one rag of
a chemise but I cannot get along with such abuse of the
children. I want him to let me take the children & go

away. I am sure I can get some kind of living for them;
but he entirely refuses, calling me a d—d fool &
threatening to "smash my mouth." I don't pretend that I
am very amiable for I am utterly sick of such
management, & when a man gets to going regularly
every morning to "bum" a drink I'm through with
him.[11]

The strain of poverty and unrealistic ambitions was
driving a wedge between Dr. Gally and his wife. The
doctor would earn $42 for the freight he carried to
Belmont, and Mat was glad to see him out of the house,
which seemed "quiet and peaceable" with him gone.
After he had returned with money from a second
freighting job—this one to Reveille—Mat paid the Joslyn
account and purchased a supply of hay and barley for the
horses.

As if matters were not bad enough, the doctor and his
Hot Creek acquaintances started drinking more than was
good for them. Hard times, the cold weather, or the
marriage of Sarah Randall to Mr. Cornell had precipitated
a community drinking spree, but whatever the cause, most
of the men were in various stages of inebriation during the
first week of February. Captain Ellis and William Smythe
were dead drunk, and on the day of Sarah Randall's
wedding, which was "coarse & rough," Garrett was
staggering around. After the doctor had returned from a
freighting trip to Morey on February 20, Mat noted that
"he was very tired & a little overstimulated—not drunk,
but nervous & restless until he went to sleep, which he
did before dark, getting up about mid-night & again at
day-break, so I did not sleep at all." Matters were much
worse the following day when the doctor was publicly
unsteady on his feet, and Mat was hurt by his conduct:

The Dr. did not go to the store before breakfast—he
brought 1 gal of whiskey with him from Belmont which
he says is Capt. Ellis' but of which he takes a drink
every morning. I cannot see how it can be right for him
to do so—he is just as well & strong as we are & for him
to spend $4.00 or $5.00 pr gr for whiskey & tobacco
(more than the clothing of the whole family comes too)
while we save every *bit* I can't see. I tore up my only
warm petticoat yesterday, to line his coat, because I had
no money to buy lining & yet he throws the money it
would have required away in a day. I can't see the justice.
. . . If this money went for any use, or if he was sick &
required luxuries, all right I would not say one word, but
for him to degrade & disgrace himself & us all, I cannot
endure—to see him with red eyes, dirty slobering mouth,
ragged clothes (which I cannot always prevent) & broken
boots & the children likewise is too bad. What if he
hasn't been absolutely drunk for a year? it is all waste &
wickedness.[12]

The terrible pall of defeat hung over the Gallys. The
doctor's claim along the Old Dominion had proven
worthless. In January, he had prospected with Mr. Gillett,
and they had found a new ledge in Rattlesnake Canyon
that the doctor was excited about. Mat simply reported
that he "thinks he has struck a good ledge, but I guess
not."[13] Her premonitions were correct and in a few days,
after more detailed inspection, the ledge was forgotten.

Mat's anger subsided markedly after receiving the
favorable news that the doctor's "'Sunday Sermon' has
very flattering editorial comments. Also a letter from Jus
H Allen of Va City is highly complimentary, saying the
various aritcles are much applauded. . . . I am very glad
the Dr's reputation is increasing for I think he deserves
it."[14]

* * *

For all his lapses and increasing frustration, which vented itself in angry outbursts against Mat and the children, Dr. Gally did not abandon his attempt to find work. In early March, Emersley, who had purchased the upper mill from Miller, asked the doctor to turn out 20,000 bricks, offering to pay him $300. The doctor hired three men to assist him, but he ran into problems almost immediately. The weather was cold and the newly molded bricks froze hard. To complicate matters, the doctor sprained a hand and was kept from working along with his inexperienced help. With the additional expense of paying the men for some of the work he should have done, he made much less than he had expected.

Emersley, who was contracting for services without enough money to cover his expenses, had the doctor making frequent trips to Belmont and Hamilton. In mid-April, the doctor was so busy and the weather was so cold that Mat felt he was being overworked. She was concerned about him, and wrote that "every gust made me shiver twice—once for the Dr. & once for myself—the coldest weather this winter & I know he must suffer."[15] As badly as they needed the money, Mat wanted him to stay home and rest. Her enduring affection for him was revealed when she learned that Emersley, upon the doctor's return from Hamilton, wanted him immediately to make a trip to Belmont. "Poor fellow! he's tired now," she recorded on May 4.

During the spring months when he was not making trips for Emersley, Dr. Gally put in a vegetable garden. By early April he had planted beets, radishes, lettuce, and beans, and in early May he put in melons, cucumbers, turnips, radishes, corn, peas, parsley, and peppers. A spring frost killed the corn and beans, but by the end of

May there were radishes and lettuce to eat.

The work Emersley had brought to Hot Creek was short-lived. What looked like the dawn of better times was simply an illusion, for Hot Creek was not attracting money because of mining booms at Pioche and Eureka. The Blue Jay mill was closed down early in March, and Zottman, one of the proprietors, turned to blacksmithing. Several weeks later, many properties in the Empire district were foreclosed. Emersley had the upper mill running for about two-and-a-half months, but when he could no longer support his mining operations in Rattlesnake Canyon, he avoided paying his debts. This meant that the doctor would not receive the $600 owed him for the freighting trips, the bricks, and his other services. On June 8, Mat stated: "We are living on scant allowance—bread, potatoes & coffee. Mr. E. is paying out no money & everyone is restless & uneasy."

The little money that the doctor brought in did not go far, and the Gallys purchased only the necessary staples. Mat had to make do with only bread and coffee, sometimes supplementing their meager fare with a slice of bacon or stewed or fried apples. A pound of good butter was a luxury. When they could afford a can of beans, she cooked them with bacon rinds to make the dish tastier. In the summer, she served lettuce from the garden with bacon, biscuits, and coffee, which made "the most savory of meals." Some poorly baked bread made her feel penitent, considering their poor diet. "I baked," she declared on July 27, "some poor bread which is a living disgrace."

In mid-August, Mat could not afford to buy sugar or coffee, and she complained on August 21 that "we have nothing to eat but beans and bread—flour most gone &

only 25¢ in the house.'' They had run up a $200 grocery bill at Joslyn's store over the preceding months, and they had to continue to purchase necessities there on credit. To appease Joslyn, James sold the colt for $15 and paid off $10 of their bill.

Poverty had many ramifications for the Gally family. The doctor became increasingly difficult to live with. Mat grew apprehensive when he stayed too long at Joslyn's store, ''which is always a bad thing for him to do.... Mrs. Gillett gave me the Pioneer, a woman's paper to read—one thing sure if the women voted there would not be so much drunkenness in either public or private life.''[16] She disliked him drinking whisky before breakfast and again at the store.

As difficult to bear as the doctor's ill-humor was the ragged state of the entire family. Mat did her best patching and repairing the doctor's coat and making a pair of drawers out of flour sacks. James walked around with painfully tender feet because they did not have the money to buy him a pair of properly fitting boots, and he was also badly in need of pants. Eventually, Mat was able to secure enough money to order boots for James and a dress for Matty. Without even the bare necessities, the offer of a piano for Matty from her grandfather was ludicrous. As for Mat, she too needed clothing, and she even sold a calico dress from her meager wardrobe to bring in a few pennies.

The family continued to suffer from minor ailments. The doctor complained greatly about an attack of indigestion, which he thought had induced cholera morbus, and a scorpion's bite on his chest elicited more fright and concern than harm. His greatest discomfort actually came from ticks, and to fend them off he "greased himself all over the head & face with bacon to destroy the gnats that persecute him cruelly—an unctious annointing!"[17] Matty, although she worried her mother with hysterical outbursts, was stronger than James, who suffered the gamut of common illnesses including a sore knee, diarrhea, neuralgia, upset stomach, boils, "nervous choking fits," and general malaise.

The social life of the village was crude. Mat did not particularly like her neighbors in 1870—the Smythes, Randalls, and Ernsts—and after Mrs. Randall and her daughters visited in January, she commented how "very stupid they are." One of them, Alice, she described as "a great goose & so plain." She relented a little toward the Randalls when Sarah, who was to marry Jacob Cornell, the butcher, needed help cutting out a jacket; and she made some sheets for her as a wedding gift. Mat did not miss the tribe however, when they departed for California in June.

Plainly, Mat preferred to keep to herself unless she really was needed. Upon hearing that Mrs. Smythe was sick, she declared that her neighbor had "a wearisome time of it." With the Ernsts, who arrived at Hot Creek during August and who had a sizable interest in one of the mines, she found nothing in common. Sophy Ernst, who was engaged to marry J. T. Williams, a successful miner and a man of some cultivation, Mat described as "not at all pretty and seems foolish."[18]

The same neighborly closeness that existed during the early years of the Hot Creek settlement was no longer evident, and Mat counted only on the friendship of Mrs. Foster. Visits from their many old mining acquaintances and friends meant more to Mat then the petty conversation of the Hot Creek women. Of the men residing in the settlement, Mat respected Mr. Williams and Mr. Gillett, whose successes and conversation she found agreeable. Williams was prepared to buy the White Pine *Inland Empire* and have the doctor edit it, as Mat explained in her diary: "he is very kind & his $30,000 makes no shadow of change in him. He offers to buy the Empire office if the Dr. will edit a paper—but I do not believe the Dr. will consider it a profitable investment for either of them."[19]

Gillett was Dr. Gally's prospecting partner in 1870, and he, like Williams, had made money from mining ventures. The doctor was anxious to please him, and he encouraged Gillett to ask Mat "earnestly & especially" to write a letter on his behalf to his estranged wife, Ruth. Mat wrote the letter only after the doctor ordered her to, but what she wrote met with so much disapproval from the doctor that she destroyed it. To keep peace, she wrote a second letter because, as she explained, "I felt sorry for Mr. G. who is in trouble."[20]

Mat had little patience with the other Hot Creek men. She listened sympathetically when they came to her with tales of woe; but she thought them uncouth and querulous and found no new reason to revise her earlier opinion of Smythe, Reno, Ellis, and their companions. She did not approve of their drunken caterwauling and considered them infinitely petty in their relationships. Examples of this pettiness abounded in Hot Creek life. Randall killed Kentuck's dog, a malicious act for which he was fined $25 in Dr. Gally's court. Wehalie ranted about prosecuting Miller for theft. Joe Williams gave his fiancée Gillett's cooking utensils, which were reclaimed by the indignant Gillett. Smythe and Cornell accused Jack Henderson of theft and fraud, a complaint that was dismissed for lack of evidence. Smythe took up more of Dr. Gally's time than anyone else, and Mat concluded that he was "a troublesome customer & the Dr. has the patience of Job."[21]

Dr. Gally recognized the constricting grip of the frontier on Mat's life, and he admitted that the camps made "the tedious days wear in and out upon a woman's listless life like barren sunlight through a prison cell." He did not write about Mat specifically, but commented generally on the pioneer woman who had "withstood the storms of the mountains, the out of door life and exposure, the scant fare and homelessness with a patient heroism equal, if not superior, to any man."[22]

A woman of Mat's delicate upbringing could not have survived the harshness of frontier life had she not been able to draw on intense inner strength. She could divert herself with household and gardening tasks, but reading was the pastime that made her troubles seem insignificant. Shakespeare, as always, came first, but there were sessions with Milton, Pope, Junius, Bulwer, Dickens, and Cervantes. Of these authors, Dickens came nearest to explaining the meaning of her own life:

> I looked over David Copperfield—now that Dickens has gone they (his books) are more than before—& David Copperfield for its wonderful picturing of truth, courage, patient tenderness, the anguish, so dull & heavy, of endurance—the sublimity of hope & the serene quiet of fidelity—will live always. Who in the world would miss Mr Peggoty & Ham from the catalogue of fond friends & Agnes that "perfect woman" & yet not too good for human nature's daily food.[23]

Mat's children had always given her pleasure, and now that they were ages fourteen and twelve, she could see that they had benefited from the frontier experience. James was tackling jobs that required a man's skill and dexterity. He worked around the camp piling up lumber, assisted Mr. Cornell with the butchering, and spent much time watching Mr. Carroll repair the mill's machinery. Mr. Page had asked him to sell his hay on a commission basis, and he occasionally accompanied Hot Creek men on trips to nearby Fish Lake, Morey, and Rattlesnake Canyon.

Matty spent more time around the house than did James. She helped her mother build a stone fence to protect their garden from the foraging cattle. She decorated the cabin with flowers, bound up the saddle, and made for her mother "the nicest yeast powder biscuit that I ever ate."

For Dr. Gally, fulfillment and triumph over poverty came from writing, and his talents were recognized far beyond the boundaries of Hot Creek. Early in 1870, his friends petitioned the county commissioners to have him serve the camp again as its justice of the peace, and there was even talk that he should run for district judge of Nye County. His letters and poems to the Virginia City *Territorial Enterprise* attracted statewide attention. The *Enterprise* praised "Singleline," who had written with "much humor and originality," was "the possessor of undoubted genius," and had a superb knowledge of eastern Nevada, "for his indomitable energy has made him traverse all the hills and valleys of that remarkable section, time and again, without having replenished what at one time was somewhat a plethoric purse."[24]

Dr. Gally's purse was as empty as ever, but work from his pen—without remuneration of course—was in demand. He received encouragement from the *Enterprise* staff, which selected one of his poems for a forthcoming volume of sagebrush poetry. Both C. A. V. Putnam, who worked for the *Enterprise*, and Judge C. C. Goodwin, who was a politician and newspaperman, helped to establish his growing reputation. His letters, poems, and stories reflected his optimism and his ultimate faith in the mines.

13

The Two-G Mine

GOOD FORTUNE was on the way for the Gally family. Ever since June of 1870, Gillett and the doctor had been prospecting in the canyons south of Hot Creek, and they discovered a promising ledge which they named the Blackstone. This discovery foreshadowed their magnificent discovery on August 28 of a ledge in Jerusalem Canyon several miles south of Hot Creek. The ledge measured between four and eight feet in width and extended 1,600 feet along the surface.

Matters moved rapidly after the discovery. A deed to 1,200 feet of the property, which Dr. Gally was calling the Two-G, was recorded promptly, and a mining district was organized on September 2 in a meeting at Joslyn's store. After some discussion about the name of the new district, they settled on Tybo. The laws of the district were drawn up by mid-September.

The discovery of the ledge created considerable interest, and everyone anxiously awaited the assay report

on the Two-G rock. Mat noted that several men came
from Austin to look at the mine, calling it

> the finest prospect they ever saw, (which seems to be the
> opinion of all who see it) & if the rock goes $50 they
> will immediately erect a furnace. They want to handle
> and desire to know by the middle of the week the figures
> at which it is for sale.[1]

By September 11, the first report from Reveille was
completed, and it indicated that assorted batches of rock
assayed at $188.50, $117.90, and $94; a second report
from Judge Goodwin indicated a similar range. The large
extent of the ledge made the assays look extremely good,
and Mat elatedly declared that "they think their fight is
over."[2]

At last, the future seemed secure for the Gallys. Two
weeks before the discovery, Mat had only 25 cents on
hand and owed $200 to Joslyn. Early in June, when
Gillett and the doctor had made their initial prospecting
tour, Mat had complained that the doctor had taken the
last of the bacon, and she thought resentfully that he
would have done better to accept an offer to make eight to
ten dollars. "Will we ever have aplenty," she lamented on
June 17. On September 1 she had the answer, "& though
we are not at this time very prosperous there is certainly a
change for the better."

As Mat received more information about the Two-G
mine, she began to hope. The doctor calculated that there
was $300,000 in ore in the ledge, but there was no mill at
Hot Creek where the ore could be reduced. Even so, Mat
was happy, and on September 16 she wrote that "I am too
much pleased for adequate expression—plainly it seems to

me the only mine I ever saw & surely it must relieve the Dr. from the pressing anxiety about his money matters which has so long distressed. I almost dare to hope his most painful days are over.''

Dr. Gally and Gillett were asking $100,000 of prospective buyers for 1,200 feet of the mine, although the assays of the ore were not yet sufficiently conclusive to determine a fair price. The doctor had to haul nearly 3,000 pounds of rock to Eureka where the ore could be milled and the value of the mine established. After the doctor and James had left on this long trip, Mat ''laid awake thinking, hoping, dreaming, & fearing.'' She missed them and worried because she had failed to mend ''the lining of James' coat sleeve—it was ripped & loose for an inch or two & will annoy him,'' but she knew that the trip held the key to their future.[3]

Anxious and nervous about the verdict on the mine, Mat filled the days as best she could. She made her own soap, struggled with the washing until the ''fingers ache—the lifting & hauling was worse than the rubbing,'' and dropped in to see Mrs. Smythe while she and Matty were looking for the colt in the canyon.[4]

The late September and early October days were hot and windy, and reinforced her sense of loneliness. ''I hope my boys are safe & comfortable in Eureka tonight,'' she wrote on September 30, ''the value of this load of rock will measurably decide our future! The wind sounds cold & wild—lonesome too.'' A report that the doctor would be delayed a week in returning home made her despondent. ''I was,'' she lamented on October 6, ''entirely discouraged—Mark Twain our only support.'' Lonely and uncertain, she and Matty walked up to the graveyard and

tried to stand up poor Crockett's headboard, & looked
long & wistfully over the wide gray valley, but no
wagon, not even a dust! Slowly & sadly we turned away
& were almost down the slope of a hill when I thought or
hoped I saw a dust in the right place.

The doctor's wagon came up the valley road and they
all rode home together. The doctor and James were
covered with dust, but they had enjoyed the trip and had
returned with shoes for mother and daughter and "a dress
of poor calico but the best they could buy" for Mat. The
rock had been left at the mill and they had received an
advance on it, but they had no idea of its milling value. In
the next several days, there was talk that Jeremiah Miller,
the millman, would buy the Two-G, but the actual sale of
the mine or of any of its extensions did not come about.
Gillett and the doctor then considered shipping the ore to
a mill near Hamilton.

To sell even a good mine required patience and
ingenuity; Gillett and Dr. Gally had to open the mine
sufficiently to establish its true value. A horde of new
trials and tribulations confronted them, but their courage
and resolution stemmed from their awareness of the prize
they held in their hands.

The Tybo Mining District attracted both prospectors
and speculators. By the end of the first week in October,
the entire district was being staked out. Anxious to protect
his interests, the doctor considered moving his family to
Tybo. Mat was not enthusiastic about moving, however,
and said she preferred to remain at Hot Creek. She felt
"we have a quiet but peaceful & busy life."[5] As usual,
she was trying to make do with what she had. Working
hard at her sewing, she fashioned a mattress cover from
barley sacks and a vest from a pair of old pants, and she

"tried to make over my old petticoat but it is all rags—[yet I] must do it."[6] She encouraged Matty to make a cover for a small mattress, and she praised the girl's effort when it was completed, recording that "this is the largest piece of sewing she has ever attempted & it has been successfully accomplished—she has been patient, thorough, pleasant & industrious a real little comfort. I don't know what I should do without her."[7]

There were even a few light, happy moments. The cat amused everyone when he pawed through the tule roof and ripped loose the cloth ceiling to gain entrance to the house. "The cat is fast taking matters into his own paws," Mat observed.[8] She wrote that "Mr. Reno got drunk & upset the Ernst wagon which contained Mr Cook & a squaw or two. They were all bruised but no one seriously injured."[9] There was a social call on Mrs. Sophy Williams, who had married their friend Joseph T. Williams. Mat had not cared for Mrs. Williams at first, but the visit improved her opinion:

> Matty & I made our bridal call—found the ladies
> exceedingly affectionate. I have been so long among
> plain quiet people that the chatter of fashionable people
> takes my breath away & I have to be kissed. When we
> came away Matty said sorrowfully "Mama, such a visit
> makes me feel so solemn." No wonder![10]

When Sophy Williams dropped in to repay the visit, staying for lunch, Mat admitted that her original opinion of the woman had been hastily formed. The Williamses sought to be gracious to the Gallys, and on James's birthday—he was fourteen years old—they brought over a birthday cake. Matty "behaved like a lady," and the doctor, who had not practiced the social proprieties in years, "ran out & hid in the back room, I not knowing he was in there, he had spent an unprofitable day & a more unprofitable evening with the politicians at the store."[11]

Happy with the serenity she had worked hard to win, the doctor's announcement in November that they would move to Tybo evoked Mat's resentment. On the morning of their departure, she did not rush to finish the wash, and the doctor was forced to do the clothes. Finally, late on a cold November afternoon, they left for their new home.

They moved into a two-room cabin that had been built on a slope encircled by high peaks. Everything about their new home was primitive. They had sunlight for only a few hours each day during the winter months, and water had to be hauled a long distance. There was no room for the stove in the cabin, and Mat had to prepare the meals outside. All kinds of visitors crowded their small quarters. Mat fed them and gave them a place to sleep, but she did not care for the numerous invasions of her privacy. Improvements were needed on the cabin: the chimney was topped out, a cabin door was hung, a chicken house and a shed were built, and the foundation for an additional room was prepared. Had it not been for the mild weather which lingered on during November, "though the ragged clouds drift threateningly across the clear blue & the pines tell threatening tales at night," Mat would have been extremely unhappy with the new arrangement.[12]

Worse than the physical discomforts was the doctor's irritability and impatience. He did not feel well, and Mat declared that he "is more querulous than old Shimmick himself—his liver is I presume inactive & he this morning took a small dose of blue mass."[13] When the doctor felt poorly, which was more often than not, he pushed the children beyond their strength and had them do the necessary work while he slept or read. In addition to the jobs which James and Matty did voluntarily around the cabin, they had to melt the ice for water and chop wood. Their duties appeared so onerous and the doctor's manner so rough that Mat cried out, "it is hard on James—the child is called upon to cut great p[ei]ces of frozen meat with neither saw nor block to go for water & wood & chop wood & save charcoal & all exposing work & not a pair of gloves to his hands."[14]

The doctor was, no doubt, verbally chastised by Mat for his attitude, for he began to work along with the children. Increasingly, Mat found fault with her husband; she refused to take seriously his groans, and she laughed at his mishaps:

> The Dr. this morning early went out in his night clothes for wood & forgetting that he had pulled in the latch string the night before allowed the door to close. In his airy costume the morning breeze nipped sharply & he begged most pitifully for admittance.[15]

Other developments could not be taken as lightly. The possibility of profits was attracting increasing numbers of prospectors and speculators to the area, including John Centraz, Charles Garrett, Rhodes, Canfield, "Joggles" Wright, "Uncle Henry," and McDonald. The Gallys had arrived none too soon, for some of the men were active claim jumpers, and the doctor was nervous and edgy. The jumpers were destroying notices and monuments, and they had squatted on some of the extensions of the Two-G mine. They worked so diligently that the original locators of the mine stood to lose everything. One rumor had Charles Garrett selling the Two-G. "Nice young man!" commented Mat, "to dispose of what he has no possession of or interest in."[16]

A few days later, the doctor and Gillett confronted Harold Adams and George Turin, who were working Two-G ground, and asked them to remove themselves. Adams and Turin, however, turned a deaf ear to the request. The situation was sufficiently nasty for Gillett and the doctor to take stern measures:

> Mr. G. told them that the first man who struck a pick into that ground he would mash his head. Whereupon they gathered their tools & went away. Mr. G. and the Dr. both dislike to be compelled to such measures but what can they do? These mean men taking possession of their property unjustly & forcibly & then say well help yourself.[17]

In another instance, Mr. McKenzie spoke of jumping a portion of the Two-G because he did not feel its locators had perfected their title. When Gillett showed him the records, he backed off.

By the end of the year, legitimate buyers were anxious to purchase the Two-G and its extensions. Jeremiah Miller, the milling man, made a bid of $4,000 for the extension and $30,000 for the Two-G. Gillett wanted the doctor to accept the offer, but he would agree only to the sale of the extension, which brought the first money the doctor had made from a mine. Dr. Gally and Gillett then began to develop the Two-G mine on their own.

So much had changed in such a short time. For Mat, the inconveniences of primitive living could be endured more easily. No longer did she have to brood over an aimless existence. Suddenly she could transmute the heartaches of the past into precious memories. The world's loveliness spoke to Mat in a sunset where "every shade of clearest color from the faintest pink to deepest

crimson & palest amber to yellowest gold & high &
serene above all the crescent moon appears."[18]

14

A Farewell To Pioneering

AFTER THE early flurry of interest in the Two-G mine, the doctor and Gillett settled down to opening it and waiting for a buyer. Four years elapsed before the Two-G was sold to John B. McGee of Eureka, and while the Gallys bided their time, they reached out for fulfillment.

During the early part of 1871, the Gallys returned to the Hot Creek homestead. For Mat, life flowed on slowly and quietly, but it was as isolated as always. The frustrations of the past were not altogether absent, but she now could look back and calmly assess her frontier experience. She renewed her correspondence with her brother George, writing in a wise and philosophical tone appropriate for an older sister. There was much to say now that the bitter struggle with poverty was over. She could reveal to him, as to no other human being, her true feelings. Of her life in Nevada, she wrote:

> I can hardly help sometimes becoming impatient of this kind of life which is rougher & more isolated than you

can guess. I could accept it for myself, but for the
children it is too bad! They have never seen a
school-house nor a church nor indeed a properly
appointed dwelling house—little barbarians they! But I
comfort myself with the thought that to know that which
about lies in daily life is the prime wisdom.[1]

George was Mat's link with family and the past. He
confided some of the details of his own family life, and he
told her about Hattie's struggle to win personal freedom
by touring Europe. Her father had married again, but was
not particularly happy in the marriage. When he died, Mat
received from George a full account of his handling of the
estate, and he discussed with her the problem of making
the small legacy support Hattie, Lizzie, and their
stepmother. The younger brother, Fuller, was never
mentioned, although George and Mat both knew that he was
working as a farmhand in Paradise Valley. Only their father,
George James, had felt the stirrings of conscience: in his
will, he directed that Fuller should have $500 and his
watch, which George Jr. would hold until "he shall be
able to give, or by some safe hand send it to him, with a
father's love and blessing."[2]

Her correspondence with George brought Mat back to
her childhood, which had been a time of books and
cultivated living. She revealed to George how much ideas
and books meant to her in lengthy comments about the
English poets who had sustained her spirits during the
frontier years. Although she missed her former life, Mat
realized that the years at Hot Creek had brought a certain
peace and serenity. She wrote to George that most human
beings, lacking warm affection, failed to experience
self-realization, and then she added: "And speaking of
sunshine reminds me of what a delightful autumn we have

had—days full of calm hot sunlight. They have had snow within 20 miles in all directions but this is Happy Valley & seldom loses its grey mat." Calm had come to Mat from "the strength of the mountain & the rest of the wide grey valley."[3]

Dr. Gally, like Mat, also had triumphed in a number of ways. His increased independence and pride were reflected in his disillusionment with politics. He refused to become the cat's-paw of other men and deserted the Democratic party in 1870. The Democrats were considering him as a candidate for district judge at their convention in September, but his name was dropped when he showed no interest in the nomination. The Republicans, quick to scent political advantage, welcomed the renegade to their ranks. Tom Fitch, the incumbent Republican candidate for Congress, proposed that Dr. Gally campaign with him throughout the state. The offer was initially accepted, and the doctor received a $100 advance from Fitch; Dr. Gally later changed his mind, however, and returned the money.

The doctor defended his politics in a letter to the *Territorial Enterprise*, stating that he did "not see the sense in following these modern dwarfs, whose banner is 'policy,' and whose watchword is 'craft.'"[4] Specifically, he saw the Democratic leadership in the South fighting for cheap coolie labor, at the expense of the Pacific slope, to offset their loss of Negro slave labor. His condemnatory remarks were reported gleefully by several Republican newspapers.[5] Some of his Democratic friends were irate, and one "malicious attack" in the Elko *Independent* accused him of absconding from the Democratic party after he realized how hopeless his bumming for political office had become. Dr. Gally retorted in the *Enterprise* that "I have been working with and hindered by some very scurvy fellows."[6]

Dr. Gally refused to retreat from his position on the enfranchisement of the Negro. Although he was prejudiced against the Indians and the Chinese, he insisted that "the negro is a citizen—as much so as you are, or as I am! That is the fact—the fixed fact."[7] For his persistent indiscretions, a Democratic newspaper, the Carson *State Register*, devoted a column on April 12, 1871, to the "perpetually disappointed but perpetual office-seeking blatherskite, Doc. Gauley, of Hot Creek," whose harangues on the Constitution in bullwhacker circles were entirely motivated by political opportunism. Dr. Gally retorted that the *Register* man needed to develop a better opinion of bullwhackers because there were more than a few who could "yoke him up and make him 'stand in.'"[8]

Dr. Gally's influence on Nevada politics counted for little, and his vehemence was largely wasted, but his own sense of civic pride was salved. Always the romantic, he dreamed of pride becoming the arbiter of the public life and releasing the nation from the grip of opportunism.

But Dr. Gally had to admit publicly that "I have cried in the wilderness, Failure! Am I much in the wrong."[9] He had abdicated from politics in 1870, but the hustings and polemics were in his blood; in the elections of 1872 and 1874, he was back in the political world with his old inimitable style. He had not forgotten or forgiven the party that had driven him out of politics or the "bummers" and "shysters" who ran it. He had good words to say about old friends such as C. C. Goodwin, J. T. Williams, Tom Tennant, M. S. Bonnifield, and Robert Mullen, and caustic ones for James W. Nye, William M. Stewart, John Garber, and Charles W. Kendall. "O,

Stewart, Stewart! rich and ripe and rotten," he opined.[10] Dr. Gally had mellowed to the point, however, where he admitted that

> other folks can run the Government about as well as I can, and ... things will, somehow, wiggle round into shape—like an improbable lot of tadpoles, in the "filthy pool of politics"—I let 'em "rip," reserving, however, my right to vote for Grant, Greeley or "gundersheimer—ven I vont to."[11]

Failing to star as a leading politician, he had to fulfill the obligations of citizenship in humbler ways. He served as foreman of the Belmont grand jury in the summer of 1873, but he was not happy sitting on juries that were bombarded by the braying of opposing counsels whose sole desire was to confuse and befuddle the panel. He proposed that the state legislature pass a bill "to prevent jurors from being talked to death."[12]

As Hot Creek's justice of the peace, he performed his duties in the vigorous tradition of the frontier judges. He lacked the fustian style of one of his colleagues, however, who fined a petty larcenist $80 because "he was a young man and I thought that it was about the fust of his steeling."[13] Typical of his alert, firm manner was the way in which he handled the case of Harry Newton and Alex Beaty. These two ranchers had been feuding for a number of months over a $6,000 debt. Beaty had plotted with a hired hand to frighten Newton into turning over the money; if Newton refused to pay up, the hired hand was to kill him. When Beaty decided against the plot, he swore out a complaint against Newton. The two men appeared before Dr. Gally, who seated them on opposite sides of the room. Before long, Newton and Beaty were trading insults, and when Newton made a suspicious-looking move, Beaty reached for his wife's satchel. Dr. Gally quickly moved for his shotgun and leveled it at the two troublemakers. The constable, who was asked to search the two men, found a pistol on Newton and a revolver in Mrs. Beaty's satchel. Matters proceeded quietly until Dr. Gally set bail for the men at $500 each. Newton refused to post bail and said the authorities could find him when they wanted him. Again, Dr. Gally brought out his shotgun, and Newton was told that he could put up the $500 or sit in the county jail until his trial. More prudent by now, he chose to post bail.[14]

* * *

Once again, the doctor found self-realization in writing. He sent letters regularly to the newspapers about conditions in his part of the country. In 1872, his mine, the Two-G, was producing galena ore rich in silver, and there was renewed activity in Rattlesnake Canyon near Hot Creek. With the country thriving, Dr. Gally enjoyed describing the terrain, natural life, and value of the interior valleys. He noted how the valleys of Nye County were sustaining cattle, perhaps as many as 20,000 sheep, and horses. "I speak," he wrote, "of good horses, not mustangs, for of these latter the more one owns the poorer one gets."[15] The drouth of 1872 in California forced stockmen to drive their herds into Nevada in search of grass. They could not find grass in abundance, but everywhere in Nevada was the white-sage, a perennial plant that could be substituted for hay.[16]

Dr. Gally appreciated the individuality that endowed the frontier people with originality. The individuality of

Gally's Nevadans reveals itself in their carriage as well as their speech. In his stories, the men of the sagebrush country seem to radiate an intense exuberance that is both physical and mental. For example, his character Big Jack Small is suffused with an energy and a confidence that draws all eyes to him. He is a teamster, a man who possesses a sharp mind, a determined will, and a firm purpose. His signature is a solemn guarantee, and in his face can be found the ''good natured shrewdness of Abraham Lincoln.'' Dr. Gally believed that Small was a typical frontier American, ''calm and humorous in the hardest struggles, through the very thrill and tickle of abundant life and pure mountain air.''[17]

But the character of the frontier dweller also contained defects, according to Dr. Gally. Egotism, lack of forbearance, exclusive self-direction, and provincial narrowness were inextricably mixed up with the realistic, independent, and self-reliant manner of the Nevada adventurer. But the greatest defect was unrestrained impulsiveness. The progress of civilization, observes Dr. Dungledaddy (one of Dr. Gally's characters), is to hammer out of a man ''the self-will he has inherited. Wisdom and patience make up the only real repentance.''[18]

Dr. Gally deplored the egotism in mining life that led to violence, but he felt that most of the adventurers struck a balance between extremes. The old frontiersman in the story, ''Out in the Night,'' admits that the miners drank, fought, and gambled; but they treated strangers with respect and would give their last penny to a needy woman. As a class, he thought that they were ''the roughest, the tenderest-hearted, most liberal and most honorable truthful set of men I ever saw.''[19]

There was a sombre side to Dr. Gally's portrayal of the Nevada adventurer, for he told the truth about their lonely lives. Prospectors who had explored over hundreds of miles for traces of silver ore dreamed of the moment when they would return home and greet the folks they had known in their boyhood, even "Tho' I reckon we'll feel like a funeral."[20] In many of Dr. Gally's poems and stories, men long separated from home and family and faced with the imminence of death fondly recall a lost past, or the news of a mother's death evokes the memory of love in a man who had shut it out from heart and mind.[21]

Dr. Gally's random observations about women reflect warmth and affection. He placed above the altar of religion "the throbbing of the full heart of flesh,"[22] and he was not offended by amorous poetry or the public advertisement of female charms. The pictures of "naked legged women" in the saloon varieties evokes from one of his adventurers the statement that these were "pictures of other men's sisters." A publican in the story retorts: "Well, them remarks is jist to the pint, but there's some difference, allus, in the way we use our own and other people's sisters."[23] And of the role of frontier women, such as Mat, he wrote:

> Damn me if I don't know hundreds of women on the frontier, in little log and mud cabins, who are called upon to bring up a family, after bringing it forth—to do more than half the work—to keep peace and preserve order in the little house—and then to comfort and coddle the old man, after keeping a sharp lookout all day across the plain without stopping her working and watching for hostile Indians?[24]

Epilogue

Success, which had eluded Dr. Gally for so many years, came at last in 1874. John B. McGee, who was superintendent of the Richmond Consolidated Mining Company at Eureka, became interested in the Tybo mines, and in 1873 he bonded a total of 3,440 feet of the best ground from the Two-G, the Hunkidori, the Lafayette, and the Caskett (of which the greatest portion, 2,100 feet, belonged to Dr. Gally and Gillett).[1] In 1874, the properties were sold to McGee for $97,000. After the division of the money, Dr. Gally's share might have been as much as $25,000.[2]

The real history of the Tybo mines began with McGee's purchase. He raised a working capital of $300,000 and incorporated a small joint stock company of three investors, two from London and one from San Francisco. The company, called the Tybo Consolidated Company, made immediate outlays for a smelting furnace, milling equipment, and the construction of a car track between the main tunnel and the mill. The bullion yield of $400 per ton proved McGee's astuteness, and the value of the property led to its London incorporation with a capital of $1,200.000.[3]

By the end of the year, the town of Tybo was flourishing, and upper, middle, and lower settlements had emerged. The company works were located in lower town; middle town was the "happy elysium of the 'soiled doves,' the sporting fraternity and the professional loafers generally, who have bid an eternal farewell to labor of any kind"; and upper town provided water and wood. Stores, a post office, a restaurant, a stable, a gambling den, and saloons were proffering services.[4]

The emergence of Tybo in 1874 marked a new period of mining activity for eastern Nevada. The mines of Hot Creek, Rattlesnake Canyon, Morey, and Belmont were again producing good-paying silver ore. White Pine, after a fire and economic collapse, was making a slow comeback. New mining discoveries had uncovered valuable new lodes at Eureka, Ely, and Pahranagat.[5]

Dr. Gally could take satisfaction in the prosperity of the region, and like many of his neighbors, he could profitably have invested in the future of Hot Creek or Tybo. Mat, however, had firmly decided that the family should emigrate to California. Her pleas might have fallen on deaf ears had she not argued for the move on behalf of the future of the children. James and Matty were sixteen and fourteen years old, respectively, and for ten years they had been without either formal schooling or the amenities of social life. Now, she pointed out, was the time to give them long-denied cultural and educational experiences and opportunities. In November, shortly after McGee had made the final payment on the mining properties, Dr. Gally agreed to move to California.

But leaving Hot Creek was not easy. For the Gallys, Hot Creek had a simplicity and beauty that Matty expressed in a poem when she was twelve years old:

> Tall and sublime/Granite and lime,
> Towering on high, Against the blue sky.
> Wide stretching plain, Untouched by rain,
> Unfed by springs, Where no wild bird sings.

A sky whose hue/Is purest blue,
Fleece clouds as white/As snow banks at night.
Meadows bright green, Where reapers glean
Full sheafs of hay/All the sunny day.[6]

Dr. Gally expressed similar sentiments in a description of the mining village on a September day:

A house, corral and stable;
And the house presents a gable
With a single door and window to the street;
A few brawny men about,
And they saunter in and out
Printing heads of many hob-nails with their feet.

There's a traveler reading news
On a box of boots and shoes;
There are picks and pans and kettles hanging out.
'Tis a mining store and station,
Place of food and recreation,
The tavern and post office on the route.

Yes, the sky is very clear,
But the scene is dry and sere,
Where the valley stretches outward from the glen;
And the mountains line the sky
Rocky, crooked, ragged, high;
And the canon stream is sinking in the fen.[7]

As the Nevada adventure was coming to an end, Dr. Gally observed: "My meeting with this State is to me a sort of romance."[8] With memories both bitter and sweet, the Gallys sold the Hot Creek ranch, packed up their belongings, and resumed the journey in the old wagon that they had abandoned in 1864. Because of the heavy Sierra snows, the wagon and horses were transported by train from Wadsworth to Sacramento, while the family rode the coach. Dr. Gally had initially intended to use the wagon to convey the family through the interior valleys from Sacramento to San Jose; but flooding had closed the country roads, and instead he shipped the wagon and team by steamer to San Francisco. Upon arriving in San Francisco and having spent all their cash, Dr. Gally loaded Mat and the children into the wagon and guided his spirited bronco team to the doors of the Bank of California on Montgomery Street.[9]

The arrival of the Gallys on Montgomery Street marked a new and easier life for them. Dr. Gally invested his money in a fruit ranch, located a few miles outside of Watsonville in the lovely Pajaro Valley. Mat had a comfortably furnished house and there found the peace she had long desired. She read her favorite authors and reflected on life, observing, for example, that "we endured for days the most depressing of *pours*, but this morning the sun is shining & the humming birds with their ruby throats are hanging & sipping at the hearts of the roses & I am wishing that I could see gilderton's golden head glinting among them."[10] She could not decide whether the orchard was more beautiful when abloom in the spring or when the fruit was ripe in the autumn. In either case, the orchard had a special charm:

> The small fruit—cherries, currants, apricots nectarines etc—is packed from the baskets, but apples, pears, quinces etc are placed upon straw on the ground in long narrow stacks under the shade of the trees so that they may be protected from rain. And until now I never had a conception of the exquisite tending & perfume of fruit—tons & tons of amber fairness, piles of pale gold with a warmth of crimson, masses of green of every shade & specimen of ruddy sweetness.[11]

She read her favorite authors—Henry James, Longfellow, Lowell, and Holmes. Referring to their works, she commented to her brother George:

> I always like Henry James—his stories & sketches, not always his travels & letters. This last story is I suppose more analytical, deeper in interest than any of his others but not I fancy more artistic & complete.... I acknowledge the consoling grace of Longfellow—he is without the grand rhythm that Bryant sometimes has & he is not so masculine & philosophic as Lowell, but he is tender & suggestive & one's ear is never jarred. And yet, though, particularly the latter part, his sonnet on summer is exquisite.... Among them all there is no name so dear to me as that of Holmes—he is the broadest & kindest of them all. I should elect him as father confessor—he is the most human & the wisest—has the widest range & sympathy.[12]

She also took pride in her husband's literary successes, and after long hesitation she sent to her brother a copy of the *Overland Monthly* containing one of his stories. "Long ago," she told him, "I wanted to send you the *O* but feared you might suppose that I desired to draw your attention to matters personal to ourselves & this I was too ill-natured to give you the opportunity to do."[13]

Everything had turned out well. James had gone to a private business college in San Francisco, and six months in school had not altered her boy. Matty was growing into a lovely woman. Mat was indeed happy, as she made clear to her brother:

> Yes, I have content. Though hot pursuit is I believe my nearest approach to that blissful state. Life is a matter of temperament & I was always uneven & irritable. I'm not a very patient old woman & yet I know my three are happier when I am—that ought to mean content. We have enough & to spare, & the first greatest use of money is to insure a certain degree of independence.[14]

She enjoyed her hard-won serenity for three years, but then fate suddenly intruded again as it had many times before. Her old dysenteric trouble took her life in the early evening of April 23, 1877. On February 11, she had written to George for the last time. Her closing words read: "We are all well—there is a cold wind blowing this aft. but for all the sweet peas, verbenas, stocks, mignonette etc are sweet with blossom." Her epitaph was plainly written on a blank page of the diary:

> All was ended now, the hope the fear & the sorrow.
> All the aching of heart the restless unsatisfied longing.
> All the deep dull pain & constant anguish of patience.

The loss was a great one for Dr. Gally. He considered the devoted love that she gave him to be the "crowning grace" of his life:

> And now, as I grow old, the days
> Come to me very sad and oft,
> Wherein I pine for homely ways,
> For voices tender, true and soft;
> And gentle hands, though coarse and red
> From heavy labor's honest wear,
> To fall like blessings on my head
> In rich, unbought, parental care.
>
> There comes upon me silent scenes
> Of days long gathered into years,
> Of frugal home, and scanty means,
> And moments glittering through tears
> Yet all of these, in life's decline,
> Draw nearer round my inner life
> Than these great properties of mine,
> Which I have won thro' years of strife.[15]

He led a quiet life after his wife's death, writing letters to the newspapers, stories for the San Francisco periodicals, and articles on fruit cultivation. Sometimes, in a sentimental mood, he thought of the sagebrush country and penned letters to old Nevada friends. In one he wrote bravely: "I was a wild 'prospector' and mountain teamster. Got over all that. Dissipations all very mild now. As a general thing I am as content and happy as any hoary old sinner has a right to expect." [16]

James and Matty lived at home for several years after the death of their mother. James was the first to leave when, at age twenty-eight, he took a job as superintendent of the farm at the Agnew Insane Asylum. The position was probably offered to him through the influence of his father, who served as a commissioner on the board of the newly built hospital. [17] After a few years, James left the Agnew Asylum and went to San Jose, where he worked in a hardware store. He married Alice Younger of San Jose and had five daughters.

After her brother's departure, Matty moved to Boston to live with her uncle George. She decided to make a career of nursing, and after training at the Massachusetts General Hospital, she worked for a number of years in Philadelphia as night superintendent of the nursing division at the University of Pennsylvania Hospital. [18] During this time, she met and fell in love with a patient whose courage and sincerity impressed her. He was the Reverend Frederick A. Bisbee, a Universalist minister. Although brought up in a non-religious environment, she married Bisbee and bore him two children; they were raised in Boston where her husband had taken a permanent church assignment as editor of the *Universalist Leader*.

With James and Matty gone, Dr. Gally lived alone. The last five years of his life were lonely, and especially after the death of his wife the drama of life seemed to end for him:

> And I have lost the essence of my will.
> Oh, no, I am not feeble yet with years,
> But, sometimes, what the women give they take.
> They send us forth and bring us back with tears
>   And keep us always living for their sake.[19]

The heroes of thought and action, the mystics and doers, the searchers after glory passed before him. He questioned whether all life is not a mere delusion and wondered whether the dreams of an old man were not as illusory as those of a boy. Finally, he came to believe that all the good in the world did not fade away without remembrance. Each generation, Dr. Gally believed, contributed its portion to humanity's storehouse.

Dr. Gally died on October 5, 1891, and his epitaph read:

> He acquired more than State fame in the sixties as a contributor to the Sacramento *Union*, and finally his graphic sketches of Nevada life found a place in the pages of the *Overland* and other magazines. . . . A man of wonderful intellect, one who has reached the full ripeness of life, has gone from this life.[20]

Notes

NOTES TO CHAPTER 1

1. Oliver I. Taylor, *Directory of the City of Wheeling and Ohio County ... as Exhibited by Census of 1850* (Wheeling: *Daily Gazette*, 1851), pp. 6-7, 49. Genealogical notes in Gally Family Papers, Bancroft Library, University of California, Berkeley. Hereafter, the Gally Family Papers will be cited as GFP.

2. Prominent in the Temperance movement of the Old Dominion, an orator of ability, and a member of the Virginia House of Delegates in 1853 and 1854, Thomas Gally died in the prime of life at Fort Adams, Mississippi, in 1855. More information on Thomas Gally is available in "Sketch of Thomas M. Gally," *American Temperance Magazine* (1852), and in a letter from Everett S. Greer of Zanesville, Ohio, September 16, 1968.

3. George W. Hawes, *Ohio State Register and Business Directory, 1860-61* (Indianapolis: George W. Hawes, 1860), p. 637; Norris F. Schneider, *Y Bridge City* (New York: World Publishing Company, 1950), passim. For information about Dr. Gally's early career, see *Courier* (Zanesville, Ohio), June 2, 1853; *Aurora* (Zanesville, Ohio), April 3, 1852; and *Times Recorder* (Zanesville, Ohio), April 23, 1961.

4. For details about the James family, see *Times Recorder*, October 22, 1950; Lemuel A. Abbott, *Descendants of George Abbott, of Rowley, Massachusetts* (n.p.: Compiler, 1906), II, 576-77; and George James's Will, July 1, 1872, County Court, Muskingum County, Ohio.

5. Orrin Pearson, *A Concise History of La Fayette Lodge, No. 79, Free and Accepted Masons of Zanesville, Ohio, Including a Brief History of Freemasonry* (n.p.: Lafayette Lodge, 1926), pp. 27-28.

6. Martha James Gally, Letter to George Abbott James, May 15, 1871, Gally Family Letters 1861-1877, GFP. All family letters unless otherwise cited belong to this collection in the GFP.

7. Ibid., August 17, 1863.

8. *Territorial Enterprise* (Virginia City, Nevada), September 15, 1870; "The Baby on the Wall," *The Californian*, VI (July-December 1882), 339.

9. Inscription to "little King," GFP.

10. J. Hope Sutor, *Past and Present of the City of Zanesville and Muskingum County, Ohio* (Chicago: S. J. Clarke, 1905), p. 105; *History of Muskingum County, Ohio* (Columbus, Ohio: J. F. Everhart, 1882), p. 207; *Eureka* (Nevada) *Sentinel*, December 5, 1871; *Territorial Enterprise*, September 19, 1870.

11. *Aurora*, June 17, 1859.

12. *Reese River Reveille* (Austin, Nevada), December 11, 1871.

13. *Territorial Enterprise*, October 25, 1870.

14. Thomas William Lewis, *History of Southeastern Ohio and the Muskingum Valley, 1788-1928* (Chicago: S. J. Clarke, 1928), I, 562.

15. Homer W. King, *Pulitzer's Prize Editor: A Biography of John A. Cockerill 1845-1896* (Durham, N.C.: Duke University Press, 1965), pp. 41-42, 44-45; Thomas W. Powell (ed.), *The Democratic Party of the State of Ohio* (n.p.: Ohio Publishing Company, 1913), I, 133-34, 142, 148.

16. James W. Gally, Letter to George James, March 4, 1886, GFP.

NOTES TO CHAPTER 2

1. Martha Virginia James Gally, Diary, February 1, 1868; December 25, 1864; and January 27, 1865, GFP. Hereafter cited as Diary.

2. *Sacramento* (California) *Daily Union*, June 28, 1873.

3. Eugene F. Ware, *The Indian War of 1864* (New York: St. Martin's Press, 1960), p. 131. First published in 1911, this work gives an invaluable account of Indian and emigrant affairs along the trail in 1864.

4. Martha James Gally, Letter to George James, April 17, 1865, GFP.

5. W. J. Ghent, *The Road to Oregon* (London: Longmans, 1929), pp. 101-02; Oscar Osburn Winther, *The Transportation Frontier: Trans-Mississippi West, 1865-1890* (New York: Holt, Rinehart and Winston, 1964), pp. 1-15. Of the many guidebooks, Randolph B. Narcy's *The Prairie Traveler: A Hand-Book for Overland Expeditions; with Maps, Illustrations, and Itineraries of the Principal Routes Between the Mississippi and the Pacific* (New York: Harper & Brothers, 1859) was available before the Gallys departed for Iowa.

6. Ware, *The Indian War of 1864*, p. 142 passim. For an analysis of the Indian problem of 1864, see George E. Hyde, *Spotted Tail's Folk* (Norman: University of Oklahoma Press, 1961), pp. 85-92.

7. Ware, *The Indian War of 1864*, pp. 183-84. It is impossible to reconstruct exactly the Gally family's itinerary of travel. They might

well have been ahead of this wagon train, although they arrived in Austin at about the same time as some parties attached to the train.

8. David Rohrer Leeper, *The Argonauts of Forty-Nine* (1894; reprint ed., Columbus, Ohio: Long's College Book Co., 1950), p. 29; Ghent, *The Road to Oregon*, pp. 134-38; Ware, *The Indian War of 1864*, pp. 191-92.

9. James W. Gally, Letter to George James, January 27, 1865, GFP.

10. *Reese River Reveille*, October 8, 18, 1864.

11. Contemporary letters by Henry J. Labatt are extremely descriptive and give a detailed picture of emigrant travel in the mid-1860s. See, for example, *Reese River Reveille*, September 16, 1866.

12. Sarah Eleanor Royce Bayliss, *Frontier Lady: Recollections of the Gold Rush and Early California*, ed. by Ralph Henry Gabriel (New Haven: Yale University Press, 1932), p. 29.

13. *Reese River Reveille*, August 28, 1866; Hubert H. Bancroft, *History of Utah, 1540-1886* (San Francisco: The History Co., 1882-1890), pp. 576-88; Leonard J. Arrington, *Great Basin Kingdom: An Economic History of the Latter Day Saints, 1830-1900* (Lincoln: University of Nebraska Press, 1966), pp. 211-15.

14. *Reese River Reveille*, September 4, 1866.

15. *Sacramento Daily Union*, June 28, 1873.

16. James W. Gally, "Ghosted," *Overland Monthly*, Sec. Ser., VIII (August 1886), 120.

17. For descriptions of these passes, see *Reese River Reveille*, July 11, 24, 30, 1866, November 9, 1865.

18. Martha James Gally, Letter to George James, n.d. (ca. fall of 1864), GFP.

19. Ibid.

20. *Territorial Enterprise*, July 25, 1869.

NOTES TO CHAPTER 3

1. Martha James Gally, Letter to George James, April 17, 1865, GFP; *Reese River Reveille*, September 23, 1865.

2. Myron Angel, *History of Nevada, with Illustrations and Biographical Sketches of its Prominent Men and Pioneers* (1881; reprint edition, Berkeley: Howell-North, 1958), p. 106.

3. J. Ross Browne, "The Reese River Country," *Harper's New Monthly Magazine*, XXXIII (June 1866), 30-31, 33.

4. W. C. Bryant, *The Silver Mines of Nevada* (New York: W. C. Bryant & Co., 1865), p. 29; *Reese River Reveille*, July 23, October 23, 1864.

5. Samuel Bowles, *Across the Continent: A Summer's Journey* (Springfield, Mass.: Samuel Bowles & Co., 1866), pp. 143-45.

6. *Reese River Reveille*, October 9, 14, 21, 22, 23, 26, 29, 1864, January 9, 26, February 10, March 13, 18, June 8, 9, 1865.

7. Ibid., May 7, 1864, March 3, June 14, 28, 29, 1865, April 25, 1866.

8. Ibid., February 6, March 6, 7, 10, 13, 25, 30, 1865.

9. Ibid., January 6, 1865, March 2, 1867.

10. Ibid., October 11, 21, 22, 26, 30, 1864, July 21, 1865, January 18, 1866. In June 1865, the school census enumerated 404 children in Austin. To serve those in attendance, two rooms were rented and paid for largely by public gifts of money.

11. Bowles, *Across the Continent*, p. 142; Writers' Program, Nevada, *Nevada: A Guide to the Silver State* (Portland, Ore.: Binfords & Mort, 1940), p. 259. At a cost of $.75, the French restaurant, run by the Baron brothers, served a meal consisting of several slices of roasted and boiled meats, vegetables, dessert, cheese, and coffee. *Reese River Reveille*, May 24, 1866.

12. *Reese River Reveille*, July 13, October 4, 8, 11, 13, 15, 27, 1865.

13. Martha James Gally, Letter to George James, April 17, 1865, GFP.

14. Ibid.

15. Ibid.

16. James W. Gally, Letter to George James, January 27, 1865, GFP.

17. Ibid.

18. *Reese River Reveille*, November 28, 1864.

19. Martha James Gally, Letter to George James, April 17, 1865, GFP.

20. *Reese River Reveille*, November 30, December 17, 19, 20, 21, 22, 23, 24, 1864, January 7, 1865.

21. *Signal* (Zanesville, Ohio), dated Hot Creek, Nevada, May 22, 1872, GFP.

22. James W. Gally, Letter to George James, March 4, 1866, GFP.

23. Ibid., January 27, 1865.

24. *Reese River Reveille*, December 30, 1864, January 3, 1865.

NOTES TO CHAPTER 4

1. James W. Gally, "Ghosted," p. 121.

2. *Reese River Reveille* January 24, December 28, 1865; *Gold Hill* (Nevada) *News*, January 24, 1865.

3. *Reese River Reveille,* July 14, 1865.

4. Ibid., January 27, 30, February 14, 1865.

5. Ibid., January 7, 1865.

6. Ibid., March 23, 1865.

7. Ibid., February 1, 8, 10, 13, 16, 22, March 9, 11, May 31, 1865.

8. Martha James Gally, Letter to George James, April 17, 1865, GFP.

9. *Reese River Reveille,* April 8, 12, 15, May 4, 8, 12, 20, 27, 30, June 7, 1865; Angel, *History of Nevada,* pp. 170-74.

10. *Reese River Reveille,* July 14, 1865; *Silver Bend Reporter* (Belmont, Nevada), March 28, 1868; Angel, *History of Nevada,* pp. 467-68.

11. Martha James Gally, Letter to George James, April 17, 1865, GFP.

12. Ibid.

13. Ibid., n.d. (ca. fall of 1864).

14. *Carson Daily Appeal* (Carson City, Nevada), August 26, September 9, 1865; *Reese River Reveille,* August 16, 1865.

15. *Reese River Reveille,* July 21, 1866.

16. Ibid., June 28, August 1, 1865; James W. Gally, Letter to George James, March 4, 1866, GFP.

17. *Reese River Reveille,* June 20, July 11, 25, September 11, 1865.

18. Ibid., October 30, November 18, 1865; Angel, *History of Nevada,* p. 346.

19. Diary, January 25, 1866, GFP.

20. *Reese River Reveille,* January 12, March 20, September 11, 1866.

21. Ibid., February 26, 1866. Dr. Gally has Beard losing his feet. The *Signal,* dated Hot Creek, Nevada, April 6, 1872, GFP.

22. Diary, February 13, 1866, GFP.

23. W. Turrentine Jackson, *Treasure Hill: Portrait of a Silver Mining Camp* (Tucson: University of Arizona Press, 1963), pp. 5-10; Angel, *History of Nevada,* p. 426.

24. Diary, May 15, 1866, GFP.

NOTES TO CHAPTER 5

1. *Reese River Reveille,* September 5, 1866.

2. Ibid., November 16, December 14, 1865; *Gold Hill News,* August 25, December 19, 1865. Judge Ralston became lost and perished in the region south of Austin, see Effie Mona Mack, "Desert Victim," *The Nevada Magazine* (May 1946), pp. 6-10, 26; *Gold Hill News,* September 20, 1865.

3. Diary, July 29, 1866, GFP.

4. Ibid., June 16, 1866.

5. Ibid., June 17, 1866.

6. Ibid., June 29, 1866.

7. Ibid., August 8, 1866.

8. Ibid., July 25, 1866.

9. Ibid., July 27, 1866.

10. Ibid., September 12, 1866.

11. Ibid., September 15, 1866.

12. Ibid., September 16, 1866.

13. Ibid., September 21, 1866.

14. Ibid., October 11, 1866.

15. *Reese River Reveille*, May 12, October 17, 29, 31, November 3, 1866.

16. *Reese River Reveille*, August 13, 1866.

17. *Territorial Enterprise*, September 14, 1866; *Reese River Reveille*, November 1, 1866.

18. *Territorial Enterprise*, May 30, October 20, 1866; *Reese River Reveille*, September 22, 26, October 16, 1866, April 20, 1868; Howard K. Beale, *The Critical Year* (New York: F. Ungar, 1958), pp. 178, 209; William Hanchett, ''Yankee Law and the Negro in Nevada, 1861-1869,'' *Western Humanities Review*, X (Summer 1956), 247.

19. *Reese River Reveille*, October 18, 1866; *Territorial Enterprise*, June 2, July 25, August 18, 23, 30, October 4, 7, 10, 1866; Eric L. McKitrick, *Andrew Johnson and Reconstruction* (Chicago: University of Chicago Press, 1960), p. 334.

20. *Reese River Reveille*, September 15, June 23, August 22, 1866; *Territorial Enterprise*, April 5, 21, June 16, August 23, 24, September 14, 20, October 23, November 3, 1866.

21. *Reese River Reveille*, September 22, October 16, 1866.

22. Diary, October 17, 1866; *Reese River Reveille*, October 18, 1866.

23. Diary, October 19, 1866; *Reese River Reveille*, October 19, 1866.

24. *Reese River Reveille*, October 29, 1866.

25. Diary, October 29, 1866.

26. *Reese River Reveille*, November 5, 1866.

27. Diary, November 4, 1866.

28. Angel, *History of Nevada*, pp. 463-64.

29. *Territorial Enterprise*, October 14, 1870.

NOTES TO CHAPTER 6

1. James W. Gally, Letter to George James, March 4, 1866, GFP.

2. Diary, November 12, 1866. One of the gentry, John H. Dennis, was the recorder of the Reese River Mining District.

3. *Carson Daily Appeal*, December 1, 1865; *Reese River Reveille*, December 1, 1865; James W. Gally, "Ghosted," p. 122.

4. *Reese River Reveille*, December 4, 1866. Mahlon D. Fairchild's brothers (J. D. and O. L. C.) were the proprietors of the *Reveille*.

5. Ibid., November 7, 1865; James W. Gally, "Shackle-Foot Sam," *Overland Monthly*, First Ser., XIII (December 1874), 525.

6. Ore had been discovered a few months before by P. W. Mansfield and Jo Pringle. The veins in this district were found in limestone, and the ore could be worked by common milling processes. *Reese River Reveille*, August 14, 1866; Angel, *History of Nevada*, pp. 516-17.

7. James W. Gally, Letter to George James, n.d. (ca. 1866), GFP.

8. Everywhere in the southeastern basin country of Nevada, new mining districts were springing up. South and west of the Danville district were the Silver Bend mines, discovered in October 1865, of which Belmont was the principal mining center. Fifteen miles north of Hot Creek, which had sixty locations by June 1866, were the Morey mines, where the first discoveries were made in 1865. Twelve miles south of Hot Creek was the Empire district, where ledges were discovered in August 1866, and a mining district formed. In the same month, ore was discovered in the Reveille Range, thirty-five miles southeast of the Empire district. *Reese River Reveille*, May 1, June 30, 1866; Angel, *History of Nevada*, pp. 516-517, 519, 523-26.

9. *Report of the Nevada State Mineralogist, 1866* (Carson City: State Printer, 1867), pp. 62-63.

10. *Reese River Reveille*, September 28, 1866.

11. Ibid., August 11, 23, 1866, January 7, 1867.

12. Ibid., October 3, 1866.

13. *Report of the Nevada State Mineralogist*, p. 62.

14. *Preliminary Report Explorations and Surveys Principally in Nevada and Arizona, 1871* (Washington, D.C.: Government Printing Office, 1872), p. 42; Rossiter W. Raymond, *Mineral Resources of the States and Territories* (Washington, D.C.: Government Printing Office, 1869), pp. 108-09. The original discoverers of the Hot Creek mines were Jeremiah Miller, David Baker, Eli Baker, G. B. Montgomery, Dr. Walter, E. G. Brown, Captain A. D. Rock, Elias Garrett, and Lafayette Joslyn. Angel, *History of Nevada*, pp. 523-24.

15. *Reese River Reveille*, November 27, 1866.

16. James W. Gally, Letter to George James, n.d. (ca. 1866), GFP.

17. *Reese River Reveille*, September 19, August 11, 1866; J. Ross Browne and James W. Taylor, *Reports Upon the Mineral Resources of the United States* (Washington, D.C.: Government Printing Office, 1867), p. 133; J. Ross Browne, *Report on the Mineral Resources of the States and Territories West of the Rocky Mountains* (Washington, D.C.: Government Printing Office, 1868), p. 424.

18. *Reese River Reveille*, September 15, 18, 20, November 19, December 29, 1866.

19. *Territorial Enterprise*, July 11, 1869.

20. Diary, December 4, 1866.

21. Ibid., November 19, 1866.

22. James W. Gally, Letter to George James, n.d. (ca. 1866), GFP.

NOTES TO CHAPTER 7

1. Diary, Christmas entries, 1866, GFP.

2. James W. Gally, "Sand," *The Californian*, I (April 1880), 297; James W. Gally, Letter to George James, n.d. (ca. early 1867); *Reese River Reveille*, January 7, 1867.

3. James W. Gally, "The Deserted Camp," GFP.

4. Duncan Emrich, ed., *Comstock Bonanza* (New York: Vanguard Press, 1950), p. 159; James W. Gally, "The Deserted Camp."

5. James W. Gally, "The Deserted Camp," pp. 5, 8; James W. Gally, "Sand," p. 404.

6. Disorderly conduct and property disputes disrupted the peace of the community. The closest civil courts were at Belmont, thirty miles east of Hot Creek. Not until July 1, 1867, did Hot Creek have Dr. Gally as its first justice of the peace and ex-officio coroner, appointed by the Board of County Commissioners. Most of the cases that came before him involved property litigations. *Silver Bend Reporter,* July 6, 1867; County Clerk and Treasurer, Nye County, Tonopah, Nevada, Letter, July 29, 1955.

7. Diary, May 7, 1867.

8. *Reese River Reveille*, January 19, 1867.

9. *Sacramento Daily Union*, June 28, 1873.

10. *Silver Bend Reporter*, April 20, 1867, January 25, February 22, March 14, 21, 1868, May 12, 1870; *Reese River Reveille*, March 9, 1867.

11. *Reese River Reveille*, January 5, 8, 21, 1867. Mat states that the doctor treated Schlieman at Hot Creek, not Reveille as the *Reese River Reveille* reported. Diary, January 3, 1867.

12. Diary, May 20, 1867.

13. Ibid., June 5, 1867.

14. Ibid., July 24, 1867.

15. *Reese River Reveille*, June 12, 1867.

16. Ibid., November 28, 1866; *Carson Daily Appeal*, January 13, 1866; *Reese River Reveille*, January 23, 1867.

17. James W. Gally, Letter to *Signal*, April 6, 1872, GFP.

18. Emrich, *Comstock Bonanza*, pp. 93, 95, 97-98, 106-07, 112; *Reese River Reveille*, November 15, 1866; James W. Gally, "Sand," p. 293.

NOTES TO CHAPTER 8

1. Diary, January 28, 1868.

2. Ibid., January 5, 1868.

3. Ibid., January 24, 1868.

4. Ibid., January 20, 1868; *Vestiges of Creation,* written by Robert Chambers, presented in 1844 a popular, nonscientific theory of evolution.

5. Diary, February 25, 1868.

6. Ibid., January 15, 1868.

7. Ibid., February 1, 1868.

8. *Silver Bend Reporter*, January 25, February 8, 29, 1868.

9. Diary, February 5, 1868.

10. Ibid., March 23, 1868.

11. Ibid., March 18, 1868.

12. Ibid., March 15, 1868.

13. *Reese River Reveille*, May 8, 1868.

14. Diary, April 10, 1868.

15. Ibid., April 12, 1868.

16. Ibid., April 9, 1868.

17. Ibid., April 26, 1868. Mat was disconcerted when she had to pay 25 cents for onions that turned out to be spoiled. Prices were extremely high on the few items they could buy at the store. Butter of inferior quality cost 87 1/2 cents a pound, and even a can of tomatoes could not be bought for less.

18. Ibid., April 14, 1868.

19. Ibid., May 1, 1868.

20. Ibid., April 24, 1868.

21. Ibid., April 29, 1868.

22. Ibid., April 30, 1868.

23. Ibid., May 18, 1868.

24. *Sacramento Union,* August 16, October 11, 1873.

25. Diary, April 21, 1868.

26. Ibid., August 17, 1868.

27. Ibid., May 18, 1868.

28. Ibid., July 3, 1868.

29. Ibid., October 26, 1868. Austin, the largest settlement in central Nevada, was reported to have had no more than five hundred pounds of flour on hand which could not be purchased. The smaller communities such as Belmont and Hot Creek, which depended completely for their supplies on the larger settlement, were in dire straits.

30. Ibid., May 12, 1868.

31. Ibid., May 13, 1868.

32. Ibid., May 14, 1868.

33. Ibid., May 19, 1868.

34. Ibid., June 21, 1868.

35. Ibid., July 6, 1868.

36. Ibid., September 24, 1868.

37. Ibid., June 14, 1868.

38. Ibid., June 18, 1868.

39. Ibid., June 8, 1868.

40. Ibid., June 14, 1868.

41. Ibid., July 19, 1868.

42. Ibid., December 20, 1868.

43. Ibid., July 20, 1868.

NOTES TO CHAPTER 9

1. James W. Gally, "The Deserted Camp," GFP.

2. Diary, April 24, 1868. Mr. Rocky was apparently the same Rockyfellow who accompanied John H. Dennis, Adams, Bell, Mills, and Dr. Gally to Hot Creek in November 1866.

3. Ibid., July 29, 1868.

4. Ibid., July 30, 1868.

5. Ibid., August 30, 1868.

6. *Silver Bend Reporter*, June 8, 1867.

7. Diary, February 25, 1868.

8. *Silver Bend Reporter*, July 29, 1868.

9. Diary, August 19, 1868.

10. Ibid., October 28, 1868.

11. Ibid., February 24, 1868.

12. Ibid., April 18, 1868.

13. Ibid., August 24, 1868.

14. Ibid., May 27, 1868.

15. Ibid., July 27, 28, 29, 1868.

16. Ibid., August 27, 1868.

17. Ibid., September 17, 1868.

18. Ibid., September 13, 1868.

19. Ibid., October 16, 1868.

20. *Sacramento Union,* September 20, 1873; *Territorial Enterprise,* February 26, 1871.

21. Marvin Lewis, "James W. Gally and Frontier Culture: A Forgotten Representative," *Western Humanities Review,* X (Spring 1956), 169.

22. Diary, September 9, 7, 21, 1868.

23. Ibid., December 3, 1868.

24. Ibid., October 5, 1868.

25. Ibid., October 20, 1868.

26. Ibid., September 26, 1868.

27. Ibid., October 16, 1868.

28. Ibid., October 28, 1868.

29. Ibid., December 17, 1868.

30. Ibid., December 13, 1868.

31. Ibid., December 4, 1868.

NOTES TO CHAPTER 10

1. *Mountain Champion* (Belmont, Nevada), July 15, 1868.

2. Diary, September 14, 1868.

3. *Inland Empire* (Hamilton, Nevada), September 28, October 1, 1869.

4. Diary, September 19, 1868.

5. James W. Gally, "The Deserted Camp," GFP.

6. Jackson, *Treasure Hill,* pp. 6-10.

7. *Silver Bend Reporter,* July 15, 1868.

8. Ibid., July 25, 1868; *Reese River Reveille,* August 7, 1868; *Mountain Champion,* August 5, 1868; Rossiter W. Raymond, *Mineral Resources of the States and Territories* (Washington, D.C.: Government Printing Office, 1869), pp. 91-92.

9. *Mountain Champion,* August 5, 1868; *Silver Bend Reporter,* July 22, 1868.

10. Diary, September 10, 1868.

11. Ibid., September 11, 1868.

12. Ibid., September 22, 1868.

13. Ibid., September 25, 1868.

14. Albert S. Evans, "A Waif of the Pogonip," *Overland Monthly,* First Ser., VI (June 1871), 561.

15. *Territorial Enterprise,* December 6, 1868.

16. Ibid., July 11, 1869.

17. *Mountain Champion*, December 19, 1868, February 6, 1869.

18. *Territorial Enterprise*, February 25, 26, March 30, 1869.

19. Diary, January 5, 1869.

NOTES TO CHAPTER 11

1. As late as February 1869 White Pine had no county organization because Lander County, with the county seat at Austin, refused to lose valuable revenues by divesting itself of land to create a new county jurisdiction. The Nye County Board of Commissioners did create a township and appoint a justice of the peace and constable in July 1868, but this move was hardly sufficient to meet the needs of the new community. *Mountain Champion*, February 20, 1869.

2. *Carson Daily Appeal*, April 27, May 12, 1869; *White Pine News* (Ely, Nevada), April 19, 24, 1869; *Inland Empire*, April 23, May 23, 1869; Jackson, *Treasure Hill*, p. 54.

3. *White Pine Telegram* (Shermantown, Nevada), June 18, 23, 29, July 15, 1869; *White Pine News*, April 8, 1869, July 11, 1870; *Eureka Sentinel*, September 3, 1871; *Inland Empire*, May 7, August 20, 21, September 16, 1869; *Territorial Enterprise*, March 30, 1869.

4. *White Pine Telegram*, June 8, 1869; *Inland Empire*, May 7, September 11, 1869; *White Pine News*, May 6, 17, 1869. For a study of the free-life syndrome in the Far West, see Marvin Lewis, ''A Free Life in the Mines and on the Range,'' *Western Humanities Review*, XII (Winter 1958), 87-95.

5. *Territorial Enterprise*, February 26, 1869; *White Pine News*, July 7, 24, 1869; *White Pine Telegram*, June 12, 19, 1869, July 16, 1869; *Inland Empire*, June 22, 1869.

6. Albert S. Evans, ''Up in the Po-go-Nip,'' *Overland Monthly*, II (March 1869), 273-80.

7. *Territorial Enterprise*, March 30, 1869.

8. *White Pine Telegram*, June 14, 1869.

9. Apparently, other towns retaliated in kind. *Inland Empire*, May 28, July 22, August 4, 1869; *White Pine News*, July 15, 1870.

10. *White Pine News*, April 19, 1869.

11. *Territorial Enterprise*, March 30, 1869.

12. In 1869, there was a population of several hundred in Shermantown compared to a population of 10,000 in the district. *Territorial Enterprise*, February 26, 1869.

13. Ibid., March 30, 1869.

14. *Inland Empire*, September 14, 1869.

15. Diary, May 4, 1869. In the entry for May 5, Mat reported that

"instead of one man there were two killed, but only one burned—the murderer has escaped."

16. Ibid., July 25, 1869; *White Pine Telegram*, July 26, 1869.

17. *Territorial Enterprise*, March 30, 1869.

18. Diary, August 3, 1869.

19. Ibid., September 3, 1869.

20. Ibid., May 18, 1869.

21. Ibid., May 17, 1869.

22. Hubert Howe Bancroft, *History of Nevada, Colorado, and Wyoming, 1540-1888* (San Francisco: The History Company, 1890), pp. 278-79.

23. *Inland Empire*, July 1, 1869. Not only was the process of extraction difficult, but the base metal ores were a milling problem. *Eureka Sentinel*, May 30, 1871.

24. *Territorial Enterprise*, July 11, 1869.

25. Diary, June 9, 1869.

26. Ibid., May 9, July 21, 1869.

27. Ibid., June 10, 1869.

28. Ibid., May 26, 1869.

29. Ibid., July 9, 1869.

30. Ibid., June 16, 1869.

31. Ibid., July 20, 1869.

32. Ibid., September 26, 1869.

33. Ibid., September 21, 1869.

34. Ibid., June 18, 1869.

35. *Territorial Enterprise*, February 26, 1869.

36. Diary, April 18, 1869.

37. *White Pine News*, April 17, 1869.

38. Diary, September 24, 1869.

39. Ibid., August 8, 1869.

40. Ibid., August 20, 1869.

41. Ibid., September 17, 1869.

42. Ibid., September 24, 1869.

43. Ibid., June 7, 1869.

44. Ibid., August 27, 1869.

45. Ibid., June 17, 1869.

46. Ibid., July 10, 1869.

47. Ibid., August 9, 1869.

48. With a few exceptions, the butchers were carrying the purchases of destitute miners on their ledgers. *Inland Empire*, September 4, 1869.

49. Ibid., September 28, October 1, 1869.

NOTES TO CHAPTER 12

1. Diary, October 1, 1869.
2. Ibid., October 4, 1869.
3. Ibid., October 8, 1869.
4. Ibid., October 5, 1869.
5. Ibid., November 3, 1869.
6. *Territorial Enterprise,* November 24, 1869.
7. *Inland Empire,* October 1, 1869.
8. Diary, November 23, 1869.
9. Ibid., November 24, December 1, 1869.
10. Ibid., December 14, 1869.
11. Ibid., January 20, 1870.
12. Ibid., February 22, 1870.
13. Ibid., January 11, 1870.
14. *Territorial Enterprise,* January 9, 1870; Lewis, "James W. Gally and Frontier Culture," p. 168.
15. Diary, April 13, 1870.
16. Ibid., July 5, 1870.
17. Ibid., May 13, 1870.
18. Ibid., August 23, 1870. Angel, *History of Nevada,* pp. 524-25.
19. Diary, July 2, 1870.
20. Ibid., August 6, 1870.
21. Ibid., July 19, 1870.
22. *Inland Empire,* September 12, 1869.
23. Diary, July 2, 1870.
24. *Territorial Enterprise,* May 25, 1870.

NOTES TO CHAPTER 13

1. Diary, September 10, 1870.
2. Ibid., September 11, 1870.
3. Ibid., September 27, 1870.
4. Ibid., September 29, 1870.
5. Ibid., November 3, 1870.
6. Ibid., November 1, 1870.
7. Ibid., November 5, 1870.
8. Ibid., October 23, 1870.
9. Ibid., September 11, 1870.
10. Ibid., October 20, 1870.
11. Ibid., October 27, 1870.
12. Ibid., November 25, 1870.
13. Ibid., November 26, 1870.

14. Ibid., December 20, 1870.

15. Ibid., December 23, 1870.

16. Ibid., December 11, 1870.

17. Ibid., December 13, 1870.

18. Ibid., December 26, 1870.

NOTES TO CHAPTER 14

1. Martha James Gally, Letter to George James, May 15, 1871, GFP.

2. George James's will, July 1, 1872, County Court, Muskingum County, Ohio. Richard Fuller James passed from notice with a misadventure. He married the niece of Amos Gustin, who was a rancher in Paradise Valley. In six months, the bride gave birth to a baby. Suspicious of the child's paternity, Fuller brought a charge of incest against his wife's uncle. *Reese River Reveille*, February 2, 1874.

3. Martha James Gally, Letter to George James, January 5, 1876, GFP.

4. *Territorial Enterprise*, October 25, 1870.

5. *Elko* (Nevada) *Chronicle*, September 29, October 30, 1870; *Carson Daily Appeal*, November 4, 1870; *Territorial Enterprise*, November 4, 1870.

6. *Territorial Enterprise*, October 14, 1870. Dr. Gally's position finished him with the Democrats, but he gained precious little from the Republicans. R. B. Canfield of Belmont had decided on C. H. Belknap for district judge, "for whose election he will spend his money freely—so I suppose the Dr. will give up all hopes." Diary, August 20, 1870.

7. *Reese River Reveille*, December 11, 1871; *Eureka Sentinel*, December 10, 1871; *Territorial Enterprise*, September 19, 1870, April 9, 1871.

8. *Territorial Enterprise*, April 27, 1871.

9. Ibid., January 9, 1870.

10. *Sacramento Union*, April 25, 1874.

11. *Eureka Sentinel*, May 12, 1872.

12. *Reese River Reveille*, August 19, 1873. Dr. Gally wrote up several grand jury indictments: D. M. Hall for murder; Alexander Mestreau, his wife, and Ah Ying—alias Wing Wa and Ah Wee—for promoting banking and faro games without a license; and Samuel Gunnison and John R. Middleton for selling the same tract of land twice. Indictments dated August 11, 1873, Belmont, Nevada (County Court, Tonopah, Nye County, Nevada).

13. *Reese River Reveille*, January 25, 1866.

14. Testimony of Alex Beaty, Richard Burke, David Moore, and L. H. Newton; "True Copy of a Letter (by Alex Beaty) Offered in Testimony . . ."; Recognizances of Alex Beaty, Mary Ellen Burke, October 15, 1872; Warrant to arrest L. H. Newton, October 2 and 14, 1872. Records available in Justices Court, Hot Creek, County Court, Tonopah, Nye County, Nevada. *Inyo Register* (Bishop, California), July 11, 1940.

15. *Eureka Sentinel,* September 24, 1871.

16. *Reese River Reveille,* June 11, 1872.

17. James W. Gally, "Big Jack Small," in *Comstock Bonanza,* p. 88.

18. *Sacramento Union,* August 23, 1873.

19. Ibid., June 28, 1873.

20. *Territorial Enterprise,* July 12, 1870.

21. *Territorial Enterprise,* June 2, 1869; *Reese River Reveille,* January 23, 1872; *Sacramento Union,* November 24, 1869, September 14, 1872.

22. *Inland Empire,* September 7, 1869.

23. *Eureka Sentinel,* November 15, 1871.

24. *Sacramento Union,* September 20, 1873.

NOTES TO EPILOGUE

1. Rossiter W. Raymond, *Statistics of Mines and Mining in the States and Territories West of the Rocky Mountains* (Washington, D.C.: Government Printing Office, 1874), p. 232.

2. McGee had to put up $19,400 in hard coin as a down payment, and he was expected to pay the balance of the money by November 1. Between the time of the sale and the final payment, Gally and Gillett were involved in a lawsuit over title to the Mayflower mine and fifty feet of adjoining ground. *Mining and Scientific Press,* March 7, 1874; *Reese River Reveille,* February 12, August 17, 1874.

3. *Mining and Scientific Press,* September 19, November 14, December 26, 1874; *Reese River Reveille,* February 12, 1874.

4. *Mining and Scientific Press,* December 26, 1874; *Reese River Reveille,* April 23, 1874. In later years, many of Dr. Gally's friends and acquaintances were associated with the development of the region: L. Joslyn prospered at Hot Creek, Bob McDonald had a sawmill at Fish Creek, Joe Williams built a substantial hotel at Hot Creek. J. D. Page was in the livery business at Tybo, F. G. McDonald had a salt works at Currant Creek, J. S. Tipton was agent for the *Reveille* at Belmont, and John H. Dennis was publishing the Tuscarora *Times* with

Fairchild. *Tybo* (Nevada) *Sun,* September 29, October 20, December 15, 1877, March 16, 23, April 13, May 4, 1878.

5. *Mining and Scientific Press,* April 11, December 19, 1874.

6. *Eureka Sentinel,* December 15, 1871.

7. Ibid., September 24, 1871. The idyllic reputation of the Hot Creek camp was shattered several months before the Gallys departed. A Chinese man residing in Hot Creek was murdered in an altercation with a man from Pioche. At about the same time, a man was murdered in a card game in Tybo. *Reese River Reveille,* May 12, 26, 1874.

8. *Reese River Reveille,* July 28, 1874.

9. *Reno Evening Gazette,* April 14, 1891; *Inyo Register,* March 8, 1934.

10. Martha James Gally, Letter to George James, January 11, 1876, GFP.

11. Ibid.

12. Ibid., January 5, 1876.

13. Ibid.

14. Ibid.

15. *Sacramento Union,* January 17, 1874.

16. *Gold Hill News,* April 22, 1880.

17. *Pajaronian* (Watsonville, California), January 4, 1886, October 8, 1891.

18. John Bisbee, Letter to Author, February 5, 1965.

19. *Argonaut* (San Francisco, California), March 15, 1879.

20. *Pajaronian,* October 8, 1891.

Lewis, Marvin, 1923-1971.
  Martha and the Doctor : a frontier
family in central Nevada / by Marvin
Lewis ; edited by B. Betty Lewis. --
Reno : University of Nevada Press,
1977.
  xii, 247 p. : port. ; 21 cm. -- (A
Bristlecone paperback)
  Includes bibliographical
references.
  ISBN 0-87417-049-4

  1. Gally, Martha. 2. Gally, James
W. 3. Pioneers--Nevada--Biography.
4. Nevada--Frontier and pioneer life.
I. Title.

        979.3/02/0924 [B]
        77-24964

F841.L47 1977   03/17/78

SUPAT   B/NA A D4-045015